Scottish Football' Guide and Yearbook

EDITOR
John Robinson

Twenty-fifth Edition

British Library Cataloguing in Publication Data
A catalogue record for this book is available from the British Library

ISBN: 978-1-86223-358-4

Web site   www.soccer-books.co.uk
e-mail   info@soccer-books.co.uk

Manufactured in the UK by T.J. International of Padstow

FOREWORD

Following the reorganisation of the higher echelons of Scottish Football in 2013, this guide covers The Scottish Professional Football League as well as the Highland Football League and the Lowland Football League, both of which appear directly below in the pyramid structure.

As in previous editions we have kept the Premier section apart from the other three Leagues of the SPFL and have included both the Highland League and the Lowland League clubs and statistics too. We have still been unable to provide ground photographs for every new club but we hope to be able to do so for future editions.

We wish to thank the club secretaries for their assistance in providing the information contained in this guide. We also wish to thank Bob Budd for the cover artwork.

If readers have up-to-date ground photographs which they wish us to consider for inclusion in a future edition, please contact us at the address on the title page.

Additional copies of this guide can be obtained directly from us at the address shown on the facing page. Alternatively, orders may be placed securely via our web site – www.soccer-books.co.uk

Finally, we would like to wish our readers a happy and safe spectating season.

John Robinson
EDITOR

CONTENTS

Scottish Professional Football League – Premiership Information 3-15
Scottish Professional Football League – Other Clubs Information 16-46
Highland Football League Club Information 47-65
Lowland Football League Club Information 66-82
Statistics – Results and Final Tables – 2016/2017 Season 83-88
2016/2017 Scottish Cup Results 89-90
2016/2017 Scottish League Challenge Cup Results 91-93
2016/2017 Scottish League Cup Results 93-94
2016/2017 Scotland Internationals 95-96

THE SCOTTISH PROFESSIONAL FOOTBALL LEAGUE
SCOTTISH PREMIERSHIP

Address
National Stadium, Hampden Park,
Mount Florida, Glasgow   G42 9DE

Web Site   www.spfl.co.uk
E-mail   info@spfl.co.uk

Phone   (0141) 620-4140
Fax   (0141) 620-4141

Clubs for the 2017/2018 Season

Aberdeen FC .... Page 4

Celtic FC .... Page 5

Dundee FC .... Page 6

Hamilton Academical FC .... Page 7

Heart of Midlothian FC .... Page 8

Hibernian FC .... Page 9

Kilmarnock FC .... Page 10

Motherwell FC .... Page 11

Partick Thistle FC .... Page 12

Rangers FC .... Page 13

Ross County FC .... Page 14

St. Johnstone FC .... Page 15

ABERDEEN FC

Founded: 1903 (**Entered League**: 1904)	**Colours**: Red shirts and shorts
Nickname: 'The Dons'	**Telephone N°**: (01224) 650400
Ground: Pittodrie Stadium, Pittodrie Street,	**Ticket Office**: (01224) 631903
Aberdeen AB24 5QH	**Fax Number**: (01224) 644173
Ground Capacity: 21,421 (all seats)	**Web Site**: www.afc.co.uk
Record Attendance: 45,061 (13th March 1954)	**E-mail**: feedback@afc.co.uk
Pitch Size: 115 × 72 yards	

GENERAL INFORMATION

Car Parking: Beach Promenade, King Street and Golf Road
Coach Parking: At the rear of the Stadium in Golf Road car park (£10.00 charge)
Nearest Railway Station: Aberdeen (1 mile)
Nearest Bus Station: Aberdeen
Club Shop: At the ground
Opening Times: Monday to Saturday 9.00am to 5.00pm.
Telephone N°: (01224) 642800

GROUND INFORMATION

Away Supporters' Entrances & Sections:
Park Road entrance for the South Stand East

ADMISSION INFO (2017/2018 PRICES)

Adult Seating: £22.00 to £28.00
Under-12s Seating: £6.00
Senior Citizen Seating: £13.00 to £20.00
Under-18s/Student Seating: £10.00
Note: The prices shown are for advance ticket purchases

DISABLED INFORMATION

Wheelchairs: 7 spaces available in the South Stand for away fans. 26 spaces in total for home fans
Helpers: One helper admitted per wheelchair
Prices: Free of charge for helpers and normal prices for the disabled.
Disabled Toilets: Available in the Richard Donald Stand, the Merkland Stand, in the Away Section and in a new toilet block at the Richard Donald Stand entrance
Contact: (01224) 631903 (Bookings are necessary)

Travelling Supporters' Information:
Routes: From the City Centre, travel along Union Street then turn left into King Street. The Stadium is about ½ mile along King Street (A92) on the right-hand side.

CELTIC FC

Founded: 1888 (**Entered League**: 1890)
Nickname: 'The Bhoys' 'The Hoops'
Ground: Celtic Park, Glasgow   G40 3RE
Ground Capacity: 60,355 (All seats)
Record Attendance: 92,000 (1st January 1938)
Pitch Size: 115 × 74 yards

Colours: Green & White hooped shirts, White shorts
General Telephone Nº: 0871 226-1888
General Fax Number: (0141) 551-8106
Ticket Office Number: 0871 226-1888
Web Site: www.celticfc.net

GENERAL INFORMATION

Car Parking: Limited on Matchdays to those with a Valid Car Park Pass. Otherwise, street parking
Coach Parking: Gallowgate, Fielden Street, Biggar Street and Nuneaton Street
Nearest Railway Station: Bellgrove (10 minutes walk)
Nearest Bus Stop: Outside of the ground
Club Shop: Superstore at Celtic Park. Also in Glasgow: 154 Argyle Street and Terminal Building, Glasgow Airport. Elsewhere: 5 West Blackhall Street, Greenock; 74 Sylvania Way, The Clyde Shopping Centre, Clydebank; 72 Main Street, Coatbridge; Unit 26, The Thistle Centre, Stirling; 30/34 Ann Street, Belfast; 125 Upper Abbey Street, Dublin.
Opening Times: Please check www.celticfc.net for details
Telephone Nº: (0141) 551-4231 (Superstore)

GROUND INFORMATION

Away Supporters' Entrances & Sections:
Kinloch Street Turnstiles for the East Stand

ADMISSION INFO (2017/2018 PRICES)

Please contact the club for information about ticket pricing for the 2017/2018 season.

DISABLED INFORMATION

Wheelchairs: 141 spaces for home fans and 6 spaces for away fans in the North Stand and East Stand
Helpers: 144 helpers admitted in total
Prices: Please contact the club for information about ticket pricing for disabled supporters during the 2015/2016 season.
Disabled Toilets: 5 available in the North Stand, 2 in the East Stand and 3 in the South West Stand
Contact: 0871 226-1888 (Bookings are necessary)

Travelling Supporters' Information:
Routes: From the South and East: Take the A74 London Road towards the City Centre, Celtic Park is on the right about ½ mile past the Belvidere Hospital and the ground is clearly visible; From the West: Take the A74 London Road from the City Centre and turn left about ½ mile past Bridgeton Station.

DUNDEE FC

Founded: 1893   (**Entered League**: 1893)
Nickname: 'The Dee'
Ground: Dens Park Stadium, Sandeman Street,
Dundee   DD3 7JY
Ground Capacity: 11,850 (All seats)
Record Attendance: 43,024 (7th February 1953)

Pitch Size: 105 × 70 yards
Colours: Blue shirts with White shorts
Telephone Nº: (01382) 889966
Ticket Office: (01382) 767039
Fax Number: (01382) 832284
Web Site: www.dundeefc.co.uk

GENERAL INFORMATION
Car Parking: Street parking only
Coach Parking: Please contact the club for details
Nearest Railway Station: Dundee
Nearest Bus Station: Dundee
Club Shop: At the Stadium
Opening Times: Weekdays from 10.00am to 5.00pm
Telephone Nº: (01382) 889966

GROUND INFORMATION
Away Supporters' Entrances & Sections:
Turnstiles 33-38 for East Stand accommodation

ADMISSION INFO (2017/2018 PRICES)
Adult Seating: £20.00 – £25.00
Under-18s Seating: £10.00 – £15.00
Senior Citizen Seating: £10.00 – £15.00
Programme Price: £3.00

DISABLED INFORMATION
Wheelchairs: Accommodated in the East and West Stands
Helpers: Admitted free of charge
Prices: £10.00 for the disabled in the Disabled Area only
Disabled Toilets: Adjacent to the Disabled Area
Contact: (01382) 889966   (Bookings are necessary)

Travelling Supporters' Information:
Routes: Take the A972 from Perth (Kingsway West) to King's Cross Circus Roundabout. Take the 3rd exit into Clepington Road and turn right into Provost Road for 1 mile then take the 2nd left into Sandeman Street for the ground.

HAMILTON ACADEMICAL FC

Founded: 1874 (**Entered League**: 1897)
Nickname: 'The Accies'
Ground: New Douglas Park, Hamilton ML3 0FT
Ground Capacity: 6,017 (all seats)
Record Attendance: 6,007 (17th January 2015)
Pitch Size: 115 × 75 yards

Colours: Red and White hooped shirts, White shorts
Telephone Nº: (01698) 368650
Web Site: www.hamiltonacciesfc.co.uk
E-mail: office@acciesfc.co.uk

GENERAL INFORMATION

Car Parking: In Caird Street Council Car Park (400 yards)
Coach Parking: In Caird Street Car Park (400 yards)
Nearest Railway Station: Hamilton West (200 yards)
Nearest Bus Station: Hamilton (1 mile)
Club Shop: At the stadium
Opening Times: Weekdays 9.30am to 5.00pm
Telephone Nº: (01698) 368658

GROUND INFORMATION

Away Supporters' Entrances & Sections:
North and East Stands – use turnstiles 7 to 12

ADMISSION INFO (2017/2018 PRICES)

Adult Seating: £22.00
Under-18s Seating: £12.00
Senior Citizen Seating: £12.00
Programme Price: £2.50

DISABLED INFORMATION

Wheelchairs: Accommodated in the front row of the stand or by the trackside
Helpers: Admitted following prior booking
Prices: £10.00 in total for each disabled fan and helper
Disabled Toilets: Available
Contact: (01698) 368650 (Bookings are necessary)

Travelling Supporters' Information:
Routes: Exit the M74 at Junction 5 and follow signs marked "Football Traffic". Go past Hamilton Racecourse, turn right at the lights by Hamilton Business Park then first right again for New Park Street and Auchinraith Avenue. The ground is behind Morrisons and Sainsburys.

HEART OF MIDLOTHIAN FC

Founded: 1874 (**Entered League**: 1890)
Nickname: 'The Jam Tarts' 'Jambos'
Ground: Tynecastle Stadium, McLeod Street, Edinburgh EH11 2NL
Ground Capacity: 17,480 (All seats)
Record Attendance: 53,396 (13th January 1932)

Pitch Size: 109 × 70 yards (100 × 64 metres)
Colours: Maroon shirts and shorts
Telephone/Ticket Office N°: 0333 043-1874
Fax Number: (0131) 200-7222
Web Site: www.heartsfc.co.uk
E-mail: supporterservices@homplc.co.uk

GENERAL INFORMATION

Car Parking: Street Parking in Robertson Avenue and Wheatfield Road but none available at the ground itself
Coach Parking: Russell Road
Nearest Railway Station: Edinburgh Haymarket (½ mile)
Nearest Bus Station: St. Andrew's Square
Club Store: McLeod Street, Edinburgh
Opening Times: Weekdays 9.00am to 5.00pm, Saturday Matchdays 10.00am to 3.00pm, Non-match Saturdays 10.00am to 4.00pm and closed on Sundays.
Telephone N°: (0131) 200-7209

GROUND INFORMATION

Away Supporters' Entrances & Sections:
Roseburn Stand entrances and accommodation

ADMISSION INFO (2017/2018 PRICES)

Adult Seating: £18.00 – £32.00
Senior Citizen Seating: £13.00 – £25.00
Under-18s Seating: £10.00 – £19.00
Under-12s Seating: £5.00 – £15.00
Note: Prices vary depending on the category of the game but very few seats will be available for most home games
Programme: £3.50

DISABLED INFORMATION

Wheelchairs: 100 spaces available for home and away fans in Wheatfield, Roseburn & Gorgie Stands
Helpers: Admitted
Prices: Please contact the club for further details
Disabled Toilets: Available
Contact: (0131) 200-7209 (Bookings are necessary)

Travelling Supporters' Information:
Routes: From the West: Take the A71 (Ayr Road) into Gorgie Road and the ground is about ¾ mile past Saughton Park on the left; From the North: Take the A90 Queensferry Road and turn right into Drum Brae after about ½ mile. Follow Drum Brae into Meadowplace Road (about 1 mile) then Broomhouse Road to the junction with Calder Road. Turn right, then as from the West; From the South: Take the A702/A703 to the A720 (Oxgangs Road). Turn left and follow the A720 into Wester Hailes Road (2½ miles) until the junction with Calder Road. Turn right, then as from the West.

HIBERNIAN FC

Founded: 1875 (**Entered League**: 1893)
Nickname: 'The Hi-Bees'
Ground: Easter Road Stadium, 12 Albion Place,
Edinburgh EH7 5QG
Ground Capacity: 20,421 (all seats)
Record Attendance: 65,840 (2nd January 1950)
Pitch Size: 115 × 74 yards

Colours: Green and White shirts with White shorts
Telephone Nº: (0131) 661-2159
Ticket Office: 0844 844-1875 Option 1
Fax Number: (0131) 659-6488
Web Site: www.hibernianfc.co.uk
E-mail: club@hibernianfc.co.uk

GENERAL INFORMATION
Car Parking: Street parking
Coach Parking: Regent Road (by Police Direction)
Nearest Railway Station: Edinburgh Waverley
(25 minutes walk)
Nearest Bus Station: St. Andrews Square
Club Shop: Famous Five Stand
Opening Times: Monday to Friday 9.00am – 5.00pm,
Saturday Matchdays 9.00am – 3.00pm and ½ hour after the
game. Non-matchday Saturdays 9.00am – 5.00pm
Club Shop e-mail: shopcounter@hibernianfc.co.uk
Telephone Nº: (0131) 656-7078

GROUND INFORMATION
Away Supporters' Entrances & Sections:
South Stand entrances and accommodation

ADMISSION INFO (2017/2018 PRICES)
Adult Seating: £22.00 – £28.00
Concessionary Seating: £12.00
Programme Price: £3.00

DISABLED INFORMATION
Wheelchairs: 14 spaces in the West Stand, 16 spaces in the
East Stand, 11 spaces in the Famous Five Stand + 11 spaces
in the South Stand. Also, 46 dual spaces in both the South
Stand and Famous Five Stand
Helpers: One helper admitted per disabled person
Prices: Concessionary prices for the disabled and helpers
Disabled Toilets: 4 available in the Famous Five and South
Stands, 5 in the West Stand and 2 in the East Stand
Contact: (0131) 656-7066
(Bookings are necessary for home supporters. Away
Supporters should book and pay through their own club)

Travelling Supporters' Information:
Routes: From the West and North: Take the A90 Queensferry Road to the A902 and continue for 2¼ miles. Turn right into
Great Junction Street and follow into Duke Street then Lochend Road. Turn sharp right into Hawkhill Avenue at Lochend Park
and follow the road into Albion Place for the ground; From the South: Take the A1 through Musselburgh (Milton Road/Willow
Brae/London Road) and turn right into Easter Road after about 2½ miles. Take the 4th right into Albion Road for the ground.

KILMARNOCK FC

Founded: 1869 (**Entered League**: 1896)
Nickname: 'Killie'
Ground: Rugby Park, Rugby Road, Kilmarnock, Ayrshire KA1 2DP
Record Attendance: 34,246 (17th August 1963)
Pitch Size: 115 × 74 yards
Ground Capacity: 18,128 (all seats)

Colours: Shirts are Blue with broad White stripes, White shorts
Telephone No: (01563) 545300
Ticket Office No: (01563) 545310
Web Site: www.kilmarnockfc.co.uk

GENERAL INFORMATION
Car Parking: At the ground (Permit Holders only)
Coach Parking: Fairyhill Road Bus Park
Nearest Railway Station: Kilmarnock (15 minutes walk)
Nearest Bus Station: Kilmarnock (10 minutes walk)
Club Shop: Adjacent to the West Stand at the ground
Opening Times: Monday to Friday 9.00am – 5.00pm, Saturdays 10.00am – 2.00pm (until kick-off on matchdays)
Telephone No: (01563) 545310

GROUND INFORMATION
Away Supporters' Entrances & Sections:
Rugby Road turnstiles for the Chadwick Stand

ADMISSION INFO (2017/2018 PRICES)
Adult Seating: £20.00
Concessionary Seating: £15.00
Under-16s Seating: £5.00 (if accompanied by an adult)
Note: Prices vary for Old Firm and Cup games.
Programme Price: £2.50

DISABLED INFORMATION
Wheelchairs: 15 spaces each for home and away fans in the Main Stand
Helpers: One helper admitted per wheelchair
Prices: Prices vary depending on reciprocal arrangements
Disabled Toilets: 2 available in the Chadwick Stand and Moffat Stand
Contact: Kilmarnock FC Disabled Supporters' Association on (01563) 545300

Travelling Supporters' Information:
Routes: From Glasgow/Ayr: Take the A77 Kilmarnock Bypass. Exit at the Bellfield Interchange. Take the A71 (Irvine) to the first roundabout then take the A759 (Kilmarnock Town Centre). The ground is ½ mile on the left hand side.

MOTHERWELL FC

Founded: 1886 (**Entered League**: 1893)
Nickname: 'The Steelmen'
Ground: Firpark, Firpark Street, Motherwell, ML1 2QN
Ground Capacity: 13,664 (all seats)
Record Attendance: 35,632 (12th March 1952)
Pitch Size: 114 × 71 yards

Colours: Shirts are Amber with a Claret chestband and Claret trim, Shorts are Amber with Claret trim
Telephone/Ticket Office Nº: (01698) 333333
Fax Number: (01698) 338001
Web Site: www.motherwellfc.co.uk
E-mail: mfcenquiries@motherwellfc.co.uk

GENERAL INFORMATION
Car Parking: Street parking and nearby Car Parks
Coach Parking: Orbiston Street
Nearest Railway Station: Airbles (1 mile)
Nearest Bus Station: Motherwell
Club Shop: At the ground
Opening Times: Weekdays 9.30am to 4.00pm plus Saturday Matchdays from 9.30am to 5.30pm
Telephone Nº: (01698) 338025

GROUND INFORMATION
Away Supporters' Entrances & Sections:
Dalziel Drive entrances for the South Stand

ADMISSION INFO (2017/2018 PRICES)
Adult Seating: £19.00 – £27.00
Under-16s Seating: £9.00 – £14.00
Concessionary Seating: £15.00 – £18.00
Note: Discounts are available in the Family Section and prices vary depending on the category of the game
Programme Price: £2.50

DISABLED INFORMATION
Wheelchairs: 20 spaces for home fans and 10 spaces for away fans in the South-West enclosure.
Helpers: Admitted
Prices: Please phone the club for information
Disabled Toilets: One available close to the Disabled Area
Contact: (01698) 338009 (Must book 1 week in advance)

Travelling Supporters' Information:
Routes: From the East: Take the A723 into Merry Street and turn left into Brandon Street (1 mile). Follow through to Windmill Hill Street and turn right at the Fire Station into Knowetop Avenue for the ground; From Elsewhere: Exit the M74 at Junction 4 and take the A723 Hamilton Road into the Town Centre. Turn right into West Hamilton Street and follow into Brandon Street – then as from the East.

PARTICK THISTLE FC

Founded: 1876 (**Entered League**: 1890)
Nickname: 'The Jags'
Ground: Firhill Stadium, 80 Firhill Road, Glasgow, G20 7AL
Ground Capacity: 10,102 (All seats)
Record Attendance: 49,838 (18th February 1922)
Pitch Size: 105 × 75 yards

Colours: Red and Yellow striped shirts, Black shorts
Telephone N°: (0141) 579-1971
Ticket Office: (0141) 579-1971
Web Site: www.ptfc.co.uk
e-mail: mail@ptfc.co.uk

GENERAL INFORMATION

Car Parking: Street parking
Coach Parking: Panmure Street
Nearest Railway Station: Maryhill
Nearest Underground Station: St. George's Cross
Club Shops: At the ground
Opening Times: Matchdays 2.00pm to 3.00pm and 4.45pm to 5.15pm plus evening matches 6.30pm to 7.30pm and 9.15pm to 9.45pm.
Telephone N°: (0141) 579-1971

GROUND INFORMATION

Away Supporters' Entrances & Sections:
North Stand (enter via Firhill Road turnstiles)

ADMISSION INFO (2017/2018 PRICES)

Adult Seating: £22.00
Concessionary Seating: £15.00
Under-16s: Free of charge in a designated area
Note: Higher prices apply for Old Firm games

DISABLED INFORMATION

Wheelchairs: 17 spaces in the North Enclosure
Helpers: One helper admitted per wheelchair
Prices: Normal prices apply for the disabled and helpers
Disabled Toilets: Available in the North Enclosure and the North Stand
Contact: (0141) 579-1971 (Bookings are necessary)

Travelling Supporters' Information:
Routes: From the East: Exit the M8 at Junction 16; From the West: Exit the M8 at Junction 17. From both directions, follow Maryhill Road to Queen's Cross and the ground is on the right.

RANGERS FC

Founded: 1872 (**Entered League**: 1890)
Nickname: 'The Gers' 'Light Blues'
Ground: Ibrox Stadium, 150 Edmiston Drive,
Glasgow   G51 2XD
Ground Capacity: 50,987 (All seats)
Record Attendance: 118,567 (2nd January 1939)
Pitch Size: 115 × 72 yards

Colours: Shirts are Blue with White trim around the
collar, White shorts
Telephone Nº: 0871 702-1972 (13p per minute)
Ticket Office: 0871 702-1972 (13p per minute)
Web Site: www.rangers.co.uk
E-mail: webmail@rangers.co.uk

GENERAL INFORMATION
Car Parking: Albion Car Park
Coach Parking: By Police direction
Away fans Car/Coach Parking: Broomloan Road
Nearest Underground Station: Ibrox (2 minutes walk)
Nearest Bus Station: Glasgow City Centre
Club Shop: Rangers Megastore, Ibrox Stadium
Opening Times: Monday to Friday 9.30am to 5.30pm,
Saturdays 9.00am – 5.30pm and Sundays 11.00am – 5.00pm.
Opening hours may vary depending on match times
Megastore Telephone Nº: (0141) 427-4444

GROUND INFORMATION
Away Supporters' Entrances & Sections:
Govan West Corner and turnstiles

ADMISSION INFO (2017/2018 PRICES)
Please contact the club for information about ticket pricing
during the 2017/2018 season.
Note: Most of the seats are taken by season ticket holders
Programme Price: £3.50

DISABLED INFORMATION
Wheelchairs: 65 spaces for home fans in front of the West
Enclosure, 35 spaces in front of the East Enclosure, 4 spaces
in the Broomloan Stand and 7 spaces for away fans in the
Govan West Stand Corner
Helpers: Admitted
Prices: Most disabled spaces are allocated to season ticket
holders and all are priced in accordance with the general
stand prices.
Disabled Toilets: Available throughout the stadium
Contact: 0871 702-1972   (Bookings are necessary)

Travelling Supporters' Information:
Routes: From All Parts: Exit the M8 at Junction 23. The road leads straight to the Stadium.

ROSS COUNTY FC

Founded: 1929 (**Entered League**: 1994)
Nickname: 'The Staggies'
Ground: GLobal Energy Stadium, Victoria Park, Jubilee Park Road, Dingwall IV15 9QW
Ground Capacity: 6,541
Seating Capacity: 6,541
Record Attendance: 10,000 (19th February 1966)

Pitch Size: 112 × 75 yards
Colours: Navy Blue shirts and shorts
Telephone Nº: (01349) 860860
Ticket Office: (01349) 860860
Fax Number: (01349) 866277
Web Site: www.rosscountyfootballclub.co.uk
E-mail: info@rosscountyfootballclub.co.uk

GENERAL INFORMATION
Car Parking: At the ground
Coach Parking: At the ground
Nearest Railway Station: Dingwall (adjacent)
Nearest Bus Station: Dingwall
Club Shop: At the ground
Opening Times: Weekdays and Matchdays
Telephone Nº: (01349) 860860

GROUND INFORMATION
Away Supporters' Entrances & Sections:
North Stand entrances and accommodation

ADMISSION INFO (2017/2018 PRICES)
Adult Seating: £20.00 – £26.00
Under-16s Seating: £10.00 – £12.00
Concessionary Seating: £12.00 – £16.00
Note: Prices vary depending on the category of the game
Programme Price: £2.00

DISABLED INFORMATION
Wheelchairs: 6 spaces each for home and away fans
Helpers: Admitted
Prices: Normal prices are charged
Disabled Toilets: Available at the bottom of the West Stand
Contact: (01349) 860860 (Bookings are necessary)

Travelling Supporters' Information:
Routes: The ground is situated at Dingwall adjacent to the Railway Station which is down Jubilee Park Road at the bottom of the High Street.

ST. JOHNSTONE FC

Founded: 1884 (**Entered League**: 1911)
Nickname: 'Saints'
Ground: McDiarmid Park, Crieff Road, Perth, PH1 2SJ
Ground Capacity: 10,696 (All seats)
Record Attendance: 10,545 (23rd May 1999)
Pitch Size: 115 × 75 yards

Colours: Blue shirts with White shorts
Telephone Nº: (01738) 459090
Ticket Office: (01738) 455000
Fax Number: (01738) 625771
Web Site: www.perthstjohnstonefc.co.uk

GENERAL INFORMATION

Car Parking: Car park at the ground
Coach Parking: At the ground
Nearest Railway Station: Perth (3 miles)
Nearest Bus Station: Perth (3 miles)
Club Shop: At the ground
Opening Times: Weekdays from 9.00am to 5.00pm and Matchdays 1.30pm to 3.00pm
Telephone Nº: (01738) 459090

GROUND INFORMATION

Away Supporters' Entrances & Sections:
North Stand and/or the North End of the West Stand and/or the South Stand.

ADMISSION INFO (2017/2018 PRICES)

Adult Seating: £23.00 – £27.00
Under-18s Seating: £8.00 (East Stand only)
Under-16s Seating: £8.00 – £13.00
Senior Citizens: £13.00 – £14.00
Note: Under-12s are admitted free of charge when accompanied by a paying adult
Programme Price: £3.00

DISABLED INFORMATION

Wheelchairs: 8 spaces available for home fans in both the East and West Stands. 8 spaces for away fans in the West Stand.
Helpers: Please phone the club for details
Prices: Please phone the club for details
Disabled Toilets: Available in the East and West Stands
Contact: (01738) 459090   (Bookings are preferable)

Travelling Supporters' Information:
Routes: Follow the M80 to Stirling, take the A9 Inverness Road north from Perth and follow the signs for the 'Football Stadium'. The ground is situated beside a dual-carriageway – the Perth Western By-pass near Junction 11 of the M90.

THE SCOTTISH PROFESSIONAL FOOTBALL LEAGUE

CHAMPIONSHIP, LEAGUE ONE & LEAGUE TWO

Clubs for the 2017/2018 Season

Airdrieonians FC .... Page 17

Albion Rovers FC .... Page 18

Alloa Athletic FC .... Page 19

Annan Athletic FC .... Page 20

Arbroath FC .... Page 21

Ayr United FC .... Page 22

Berwick Rangers FC .... Page 23

Brechin City FC .... Page 24

Clyde FC .... Page 25

Cowdenbeath FC .... Page 26

Dumbarton FC .... Page 27

Dundee United FC............. Page 28

Dunfermline Athletic FC .. Page 29

East Fife FC .... Page 30

Edinburgh City FC .... Page 31

Elgin City FC .... Page 32

Falkirk FC.......................... Page 33

Forfar Athletic FC .... Page 34

Greenock Morton FC .... Page 35

Inverness Cal. Thistle FC .. Page 36

Livingston FC .... Page 37

Montrose FC .... Page 38

Peterhead FC .... Page 39

Queen of the South FC..... Page 40

Queen's Park FC .... Page 41

Raith Rovers FC .... Page 42

Stenhousemuir FC............ Page 43

Stirling Albion FC .... Page 44

St. Mirren FC .... Page 45

Stranraer FC...................... Page 46

AIRDRIEONIANS FC

Founded: 1965 (**Entered League**: 1966)
Former Name: Clydebank FC and Airdrie United FC
Ground: Excelsior Stadium, Broomfield Park,
Craigneuk Avenue, Airdrie   ML6 8QZ
Ground Capacity: 9,843 (All seats)
Record Attendance: 9,612

Pitch Size: 115 × 71 yards
Colours: White shirts with Red diamond, White shorts
Telephone N°: 07710 230775
Ticket Office: 07710 230775
Fax Number: (0141) 221-1497
Web Site: www.airdriefc.com

GENERAL INFORMATION
Car Parking: Behind all the Stands
Coach Parking: Behind the East Stand
Nearest Railway Station: Drumgelloch (½ mile)
Nearest Bus Station: Gartlea – Airdrie Town Centre
Club Shop: At the ground
Opening Times: Opens at 12.00pm on Home Matchdays
and Sunday 2.00pm – 4.00pm
Telephone N°: 07710 230775

GROUND INFORMATION
Away Supporters' Entrances & Sections:
East and South Stands

ADMISSION INFO (2017/2018 PRICES)
Adult Seating: £16.00
Under-16s Seating: £7.00
Senior Citizen Seating: £10.00
Note: Parent and Child tickets are priced at £20.00

DISABLED INFORMATION
Wheelchairs: Spaces available for home and away fans
accommodated in the front sections
Helpers: One admitted per disabled supporter
Prices: Each disabled supporter with a helper are admitted
for half-price
Disabled Toilets: Available in all the stands
Contact: 07800 575729   (Bookings are preferable)

Travelling Supporters' Information:
Routes: From the East: Exit the M8 at Junction 6 and take the A73 (signposted for Cumbernauld). Pass through Chapelhall into Airdrie and turn right into Petersburn Road – the ground is on the left; From the West: Take the A8 to the Chapelhall turn-off for Chapelhall. Join the A73 at Chapelhall, then as above.

ALBION ROVERS FC

Founded: 1882 (Entered League: 1903)
Nickname: 'Wee Rovers'
Ground: Cliftonhill Stadium, Main Street, Coatbridge, Lanarkshire ML5 3RB
Ground Capacity: 1,238
Seating Capacity: 538
Record Attendance: 27,381 (8th February 1936)

Pitch Size: 110 × 72 yards
Colours: Red and Yellow shirts with Red shorts
Telephone Nº: (01236) 606334
Ticket Office: (01236) 606334
Fax Number: (01236) 606334
Web Site: www.albionroversfc.co.uk

GENERAL INFORMATION

Car Parking: Street parking and Albion Street
Coach Parking: Street parking only
Nearest Railway Station: Coatdyke (10 minutes walk)
Nearest Bus Station: Coatbridge
Club Shop: At the ground
Opening Times: One hour before each home match
Telephone Nº: (01236) 606334

GROUND INFORMATION

Away Supporters' Entrances & Sections:
Main Street entrance for the Main Street Area

ADMISSION INFO (2017/2018 PRICES)

Adult Standing: £14.00
Adult Seating: £14.00
Student/Senior Citizen Standing/Seating: £5.00
Ages 13 to 16 Standing/Seating: £2.00
Under-13s Standing/Seating: Free of charge
Programme Price: £2.00

DISABLED INFORMATION

Wheelchairs: Approximately 30 spaces available in the Disabled Area
Helpers: Admitted
Prices: Normal prices for the disabled. Helpers free of charge
Disabled Toilets: Available at the East End of the Ground
Contact: (01236) 606334 (Bookings are advisable)

Travelling Supporters' Information:
Routes: From the East or West: Take the A8/M8 to the Shawhead Interchange then follow the A725 to the Town Centre. Follow A89 signs towards Airdrie at the roundabout, the ground is then on the left; From the South: Take the A725 from Bellshill/Hamilton/Motherwell/M74 to Coatbridge. Follow the A89 signs towards Airdrie at the roundabout, the ground is then on the left; From the North: Take the A73 to Airdrie then follow signs for the A8010 to Coatbridge. Join the A89 and the ground is one mile on the right.

ALLOA ATHLETIC FC

Founded: 1878 (**Entered League**: 1921)
Nickname: 'The Wasps'
Ground: The Indodrill Stadium, Clackmannan Road, Alloa   FK10 1RY
Ground Capacity: 3,100
Seating Capacity: 900
Record Attendance: 13,000 (26th February 1939)

Pitch Size: 110 × 75 yards
Colours: Gold and Black shirts with Black shorts
Telephone Nº: (01259) 722695
Ticket Office: (01259) 722695
Fax Number: (01259) 210886
Web Site: www.alloaathletic.co.uk
E-mail: fcadmin@alloaathletic.co.uk

GENERAL INFORMATION

Car Parking: A Car Park is adjacent to the ground
Coach Parking: By Police Direction
Nearest Railway Station: Alloa
Nearest Bus Station: Alloa
Club Shop: At the ground
Opening Times: Matchdays only 1.30pm to 5.00pm
Telephone Nº: (01259) 722695

GROUND INFORMATION

Away Supporters' Entrances & Sections:
Hilton Road entrance for the Hilton Road Side

ADMISSION INFO (2017/2018 PRICES)

Adult Standing: £16.00
Adult Seating: £16.00
Senior Citizen Standing/Seating: £8.00
Under-16s Standing/Seating: £4.00
Programme Price: £2.00

DISABLED INFORMATION

Wheelchairs: Accommodated in the Disabled Section underneath the Main Stand
Helpers: Admitted
Prices: Free of charge for the disabled and helpers
Disabled Toilets: One available in both the Main Stand and the away supporters' section
Contact: (01259) 722695   (Bookings are not necessary)

Travelling Supporters' Information:
Routes: From the South and East: Take the M74 to the M80 and exit at Junction 9 following the A907 into Alloa. Continue over two roundabouts passing the brewery and Town Centre. The Ground is on the left-hand side of the road.

ANNAN ATHLETIC FC

Founded: 1942
Former Names: Solway Star FC
Nickname: 'Galabankies'
Ground: Galabank, North Street, Annan, Dumfries & Galloway   DG12 5DQ
Record Attendance: 2,514
Pitch Size: 110 × 66 yards

Ground Capacity: 2,514
Seating Capacity: 474
Colours: Gold shirts with Black shorts and Gold socks
Telephone Nº: (01461) 204108
Fax Number: (01461) 204108
Web Site: www.annanathleticfc.com
E-mail: annanathleticfc1@btinternet.com

GENERAL INFORMATION
Car Parking: Available at the ground
Coach Parking: Available at the ground
Nearest Railway Station: Annan
Nearest Bus Station: Annan
Club Shop: At the ground
Opening Times: Saturdays between 3.00pm and 6.00pm
Telephone Nº: (01461) 204108

GROUND INFORMATION
Away Supporters' Entrances & Sections:
North Stand

ADMISSION INFO (2017/2018 PRICES)
Adult Standing: £10.00   **Adult Seating**: £10.00
Child Standing: £5.00   **Child Seating**: £5.00
Note: Under-12s are admitted free of charge when accompanied by a paying adult
Programme Price: £2.00

DISABLED INFORMATION
Wheelchairs: Accommodated
Helpers: Please phone the club for details
Prices: Please phone the club for details
Disabled Toilets: Available
Contact: (01461) 204108   (Bookings are necessary)

Travelling Supporters' Information:
Routes: From the East: Take the A75 to Annan. Approaching Annan, exit onto the B6357 (Stapleton Road) and after ¾ mile take the second exit at the roundabout into Scotts Street. Continue into Church Street and High Street. Turn right into Lady Street (B722) and following along into North Street for the ground; From the West: Take the A75 to Annan and turn right onto the B721 through Howes and into High Street in Annan (1 mile). After about 300 yards turn left into Lady Street. Then as above.

ARBROATH FC

Founded: 1878 (**Entered League**: 1902)
Nickname: 'The Red Lichties'
Ground: Gayfield Park, Arbroath   DD11 1QB
Ground Capacity: 6,600
Seating Capacity: 876
Record Attendance: 13,510 (23rd February 1952)

Pitch Size: 115 × 71 yards
Colours: Maroon shirts and shorts
Telephone Nº: (01241) 872157
Ticket Office: (01241) 872157
Fax Number: (01241) 431125
Web Site: www.arbroathfc.co.uk

GENERAL INFORMATION

Car Parking: Car Park in Queen's Drive
Coach Parking: Car Park in Queen's Drive
Nearest Railway Station: Arbroath (15 minutes walk)
Nearest Bus Station: Arbroath (10 minutes walk)
Club Shop: At the ground
Opening Times: Matchdays only 2.00pm – 5.00pm
Telephone Nº: (01241) 872157

GROUND INFORMATION

Away Supporters' Entrances & Sections:
Queen's Drive End

ADMISSION INFO (2017/2018 PRICES)

Adult Standing: £14.00
Adult Seating: £14.00
Concessionary Standing: £8.00
Concessionary Seating: £8.00
Family Ticket: 1 adult + 1 child £15.00
Programme Price: £2.00

DISABLED INFORMATION

Wheelchairs: 6 spaces available at both of the West and
East Ends of the Main Stand
Helpers: Admitted
Prices: Normal prices for the disabled. Free for helpers
Disabled Toilets: Two available at the rear of the Stand
Contact: (01241) 872157   (Bookings are not necessary)

Travelling Supporters' Information:
Routes: From Dundee and the West: Take the A92 (Coast Road). On entering Arbroath, pass under the Railway Line and the
ground is on the right-hand side; From Stonehaven/Montrose: Take the A92, pass through Arbroath, go past the Harbour and
the ground is on the left-hand side.

AYR UNITED FC

Founded: 1910 (**Entered League**: 1910)
Former Names: Formed by the amagamation of Ayr Parkhouse FC and Ayr FC in 1910
Nickname: 'The Honest Men'
Ground: Somerset Park, Tryfield Place, Ayr, KA8 9NB
Ground Capacity: 10,185
Seating Capacity: 1,500

Record Attendance: 25,225 (13th September 1969)
Pitch Size: 110 × 72 yards
Colours: White and Black hooped shirts, Black shorts
Telephone/Ticket Office Nº: (01292) 263435
Fax Number: (01292) 281314
Web site: www.ayrunitedfc.co.uk
E-mail: info@ayrunitedfc.co.uk

GENERAL INFORMATION

Car Parking: Craigie Car Park, Ayr Racecourse and Somerset Road Car Park
Coach Parking: Craigie Car Park
Nearest Railway Station: Ayr or Newton-on-Ayr (both stations are 10 minutes walk)
Nearest Bus Station: Sandgate, Ayr
Club Shop: At the ground
Opening Times: Monday to Friday 12.00pm to 4.00pm and Matchdays from 12.00pm to kick-off
Telephone Nº: (01292) 263435

GROUND INFORMATION

Away Supporters' Entrances & Sections:
Turnstiles 1-7 for the Railway End (covered terrace) + turnstiles 9-10 for Main Stand accommodation

ADMISSION INFO (2017/2018 PRICES)

Adult Standing: £16.00
Adult Seating: £16.00
Student/Senior Citizen Standing: £10.00
Student/Senior Citizen Seating: £10.00
Under-18s Standing/Seating: £5.00
Programme Price: £2.00

DISABLED INFORMATION

Wheelchairs: 24 spaces are available in the Disabled Area beneath the Family Stand
Helpers: One admitted per wheelchair
Prices: Free for one wheelchair plus helper
Disabled Toilets: Available in the Disabled Area
Are Bookings Necessary: Only for all-ticket games
Contact: (01292) 263435

Travelling Supporters' Information:
Routes: Make for the A77 Ring Road around Ayr, exit via Whitletts Roundabout onto the A719 and follow the road towards Ayr. Just past the end of the racecourse, turn right at the traffic lights into Burnett Terrace, a sharp left and then right takes you into Somerset Road for the ground. (For car parking on Matchdays turn left at the traffic lights and then right 50 yards on into Craigie Park or on Somerset Road just past the ground on the left into Somerset Road car park).

BERWICK RANGERS FC

Founded: 1881 (**Entered League**: 1951)
Nickname: 'The Borderers'
Ground: Shielfield Park, Shielfield Terrace,
Tweedmouth, Berwick-upon-Tweed TD15 2EF
Ground Capacity: 4,099
Seating Capacity: 1,221
Record Attendance: 13,365 (28th January 1967)
Pitch Size: 110 × 70 yards

Colours: Black and Gold Striped shirts, Black shorts
Telephone Nº: (01289) 307424
Ticket Office: (01289) 307424
Web Site: www.berwickrangers.com
E-mail: club@berwickrangers.com

GENERAL INFORMATION

Car Parking: Large Car Park at the ground
Coach Parking: At the ground
Nearest Railway Station: Berwick-upon-Tweed (1½ miles)
Nearest Bus Station: Berwick Town Centre (1 mile)
Club Shop: Inside the Stadium
Opening Times: Matchdays Only (+ On-line sales)
Telephone Nº: (01289) 307424

GROUND INFORMATION

Away Supporters' Entrances & Sections:
Shielfield Terrace entrance for the Popular Side Terrace (Gates
A or B), Gate B for Main Stand accommodation. Gate A is
only used for selected matches.

ADMISSION INFO (2017/2018 PRICES)

Adult Standing: £12.00
Adult Seating: £12.00
Concessionary Seating/Standing: £7.00
Under-16s Seating/Standing: Usually free for League
games. Please check with the club for further information.
Programme Price: £2.50

DISABLED INFORMATION

Wheelchairs: Accommodated in the disabled section
Helpers: Admitted with wheelchair disabled
Prices: Fans with disabilities are admitted free of charge
when bookings are made in advance
Disabled Toilets: Available between the turnstiles and the
Grandstand entrance and behind the covered terracing.
Also available in the Black & Gold Pub by the car park
Contact: (01289) 307424 (Bookings are recommended)

Travelling Supporters' Information:
Routes: From the North: Take the A1 (Berwick Bypass), cross the new road-bridge then take the 1st exit at the roundabout.
Carry on for approximately ¼ mile to the next roundabout, go straight across then continue for approximately ¼ mile into
Shielfield Terrace. Turn left and the ground is on the left; From the South: Take the A1 Bypass and continue across the first
roundabout signposted Scremerston/Tweedmouth and then on for 1 mile. At the crossroads/junction take B6354 'Spittal' Road
right and continue for approx. 1 mile until the road becomes Shielfield Terrace. The ground is on the left in Shielfield Terrace.

BRECHIN CITY FC

Founded: 1906 (**Entered League:** 1923)
Nickname: 'The City'
Ground: Glebe Park, Trinity Road, Brechin, Angus, DD9 6BJ
Ground Capacity: 3,960
Seating Capacity: 1,519
Record Attendance: 9,123 (3rd February 1973)

Pitch Size: 110 × 67 yards
Colours: Red and White shirts and shorts
Telephone Nº: (01356) 622856
Ticket Office: (01356) 622856
Fax Number: (01356) 625667
Secretary's Number: 07810 226224
Web Site: www.brechincity.com

GENERAL INFORMATION
Car Parking: Small Car Park at the ground and street parking
Coach Parking: Street parking
Nearest Railway Station: Montrose (8 miles)
Nearest Bus Station: Brechin
Club Shop: At the ground
Opening Times: Matchdays Only
Telephone Nº: (01356) 622856

GROUND INFORMATION
Away Supporters' Entrances & Sections:
Main Stand – Trinity Road End

ADMISSION INFO (2017/2018 PRICES)
Adult Standing: £13.00
Adult Seating: £13.00
Concessionary Standing: £7.00
Concessionary Seating: £7.00
Parent & Child Ticket: £16.00 (additional children are admitted for £2.00 each)
Programme Price: £2.00

DISABLED INFORMATION
Wheelchairs: 10 spaces each for home and away fans
Helpers: Please phone the club for details
Prices: Please phone the club for details
Disabled Toilets: Two available in the Covered Enclosure
Contact: (01356) 622856 (Bookings are not necessary)

Travelling Supporters' Information:
Routes: From the South and West: Take the M90 to the A94 and continue along past the first 'Brechin' turn-off. Take the second turn signposted 'Brechin'. On entering Brechin, the ground is on the left-hand side of the road between some houses.

CLYDE FC

Founded: 1877 (**Entered League**: 1906)
Nickname: 'Bully Wee'
Ground: Broadwood Stadium, Ardgoil Drive, Cumbernauld, Glasgow   G68 9NE
Ground Capacity: 8,200 (all seats)
Record Attendance: 8,000 (14th August 1996)
Pitch Size: 115 × 75 yards

Colours: White Shirts with Black piping, Black shorts
Telephone Nº: (01236) 451511
Ticket Office: (01236) 451511
Fax Number: (01236) 733490
Web Site: www.clydefc.co.uk
E-mail: info@clydefc.co.uk

GENERAL INFORMATION

Car Parking: Behind the Main and West Stands (200 yards)
Coach Parking: Behind the Main Stand
Nearest Railway Station: Croy (1½ miles)
Nearest Bus Station: Cumbernauld Town Centre
Club Shop: At the ground
Opening Times: One hour before and after the match
Telephone Nº: (01236) 451511

GROUND INFORMATION

Away Supporters' Entrances & Sections:
West Stand Turnstile for the West Stand area

ADMISSION INFO (2017/2018 PRICES)

Adult Seating: £13.00
Under-18s Seating: £8.00
Concessionary Seating: £8.00
Note: Under-12s are admitted free with a paying adult
Programme Price: £2.50

DISABLED INFORMATION

Wheelchairs: 10 spaces each for home and away fans accommodated in front sections of each stand
Helpers: One helper admitted per wheelchair
Prices: Free of charge for the disabled and helpers
Disabled Toilets: 4 available in the Main and West Stands
Contact: (01236) 451511   (Bookings are not necessary)

Travelling Supporters' Information:
Routes: From all Parts: Exit the A80 at Broadwood Junction and follow the signs for Broadwood. The ground is signposted from the next roundabout.

COWDENBEATH FC

Founded: 1880 (**Entered League**: 1905)
Nickname: 'Cowden' 'Blue Brazil" 'The Miners'
Ground: Central Park, High Street, Cowdenbeath KY4 9QQ
Ground Capacity: 4,370 **Seating Capacity**: 1,431
Record Attendance: 25,586 (21st September 1949)
Pitch Size: 104 × 66 yards

Colours: Shirts are Royal Blue with White trim, Shorts are White
Telephone N°: (01383) 610166
Ticket Office: (01383) 610166
Fax Number: (01383) 512132
Web Site: www.cowdenbeathfc.com
E-mail: office@cowdenbeathfc.com

GENERAL INFORMATION

Car Parking: Car Park at the ground and Stenhouse Street (200 yards). A total of 200 spaces are available
Coach Parking: King Street and Rowan Terrace
Nearest Railway Station: Cowdenbeath (400 yards)
Nearest Bus Station: Cowdenbeath (Bus Stop at ground)
Club Shop: At the ground
Opening Times: Weekdays 9.00am to 5.00pm and Matchdays 10.00am to 5.00pm
Telephone N°: (01383) 610166

GROUND INFORMATION

Away Supporters' Entrances & Sections:
High Street end of the ground

ADMISSION INFO (2017/2018 PRICES)

Adult Standing: £12.00
Adult Seating: £12.00
Child Standing/Seating: £6.00 (Ages 16 and under)
Senior Citizen Standing/Seating: £6.00
Note: Family tickets are also available
Programme Price: £2.00

DISABLED INFORMATION

Wheelchairs: 6 spaces each for home and away fans
Helpers: Please phone the club for information
Prices: Normal prices for disabled fans but free for helpers
Disabled Toilets: 1 Ladies, 1 Gents and 1 Unisex available
Contact: (01383) 610166 (Bookings are necessary)

Travelling Supporters' Information:
Routes: Exit the M90 at Junction 3 for Dunfermline. Take the Dual Carriageway to Cowdenbeath and follow straight on into the High Street. The ground is situated on the first left turn in the High Street.

DUMBARTON FC

Founded: 1872 (**Entered League:** 1890)
Nickname: 'Sons'
Ground: YOUR Radio 103fm Stadium, Castle Road, Dumbarton G82 1JJ
Ground Capacity: 2,046 (All seats)
Record Attendance: 2,035 (27th January 2001)
Pitch Size: 110 × 72 yards

Colours: All White shirts and shorts
Telephone Nº: (01389) 762569
Ticket Office: (01389) 762569
Web Site: www.dumbartonfootballclub.com
E-mail: enquiries@dumbartonfc.com

GENERAL INFORMATION
Car Parking: 400 spaces available at the ground
Coach Parking: At the ground
Nearest Railway Station: Dumbarton East
Nearest Bus Station: Dumbarton
Club Shop: At the ground
Opening Times: Monday, Wednesday and Friday 9.30am to 3.30pm plus Saturday matchdays 11.00am to 5.00pm
Telephone Nº: (01389) 762569

GROUND INFORMATION
Away Supporters' Entrances & Sections:
West Section

ADMISSION INFO (2017/2018 PRICES)
Adult Seating: £20.00 – £22.00
Concessionary Seating: £12.00 – £14.00
Family Ticket: £24.00 – £30.00
Programme Price: £2.50

DISABLED INFORMATION
Wheelchairs: Approximately 24 spaces available in the disabled area
Helpers: Please phone the club for information
Prices: Please phone the club for information
Disabled Toilets: Available
Contact: (01389) 762569   (Bookings are necessary)

Travelling Supporters' Information:
Routes: The ground is situated just by Dumbarton Castle. Take the A814 into Dumbarton and follow the brown signs for the Castle to find the ground.

DUNDEE UNITED FC

Founded: 1909 (**Entered League**: 1910)
Former Names: Dundee Hibernians FC
Nickname: 'The Terrors'
Ground: Tannadice Park, Tannadice Street, Dundee, DD3 7JW
Ground Capacity: 14,223 (all seats)
Record Attendance: 28,000 (November 1966)

Pitch Size: 110 × 72 yards
Colours: Tangerine shirts with Black shorts
Telephone Nº: (01382) 833166
Ticket Office: (01382) 833166
Fax Number: (01382) 889398
Web Site: www.dufc.co
E-mail: admin@dundeeunitedfc.co.uk

GENERAL INFORMATION

Car Parking: Street Parking only
Coach Parking: CA Arena (home coaches)
Nearest Railway Station: Dundee (20 minutes walk)
Nearest Bus Station: Dundee
Club Shop: In Tannadice Street
Opening Times: Monday to Friday 9.00am to 5.00pm. Saturdays (away matches) 9.00am–1.00pm. Saturday/Sunday matchdays 9.00am to kick-off then 30 minutes after the game.
Telephone Nº: (01382) 833166

GROUND INFORMATION

Away Supporters' Entrances & Sections:
Turnstiles 7-16 for Jerry Kerr Stand & Jim McLean Fair Play Stand

ADMISSION INFO (2017/2018 PRICES)

Adult Seating: £20.00 – £22.00
Concessionary Seating: £10.00 – £13.00
Note: Prices vary depending on the category of the game
Programme Price: £3.00

DISABLED INFORMATION

Wheelchairs: Accommodated in the George Fox Stand, the Eddie Thompson Stand and Jim McLean Fair Play Stand.
Helpers: Please phone the club for details
Prices: Please phone the club for details
Disabled Toilets: Available in the George Fox Stand, the Eddie Thompson Stand and Jim McLean Fair Play Stand.
Contact: (01382) 833166 (Bookings are necessary)

Travelling Supporters' Information:
Routes: From the South or West: Travel via Perth and take the A90 to Dundee. Once in Dundee join the Kingsway (ring road) and follow until the third exit marked "Football Traffic", then turn right onto Old Glamis Road. Follow the road to join Provost Road then turn left into Sandeman Street for the ground; From the North: Follow the A90 from Aberdeen and join the Kingsway (ring road). At the first set of traffic lights turn right into Clepington Road and follow into Arklay Street before turning right into Tannadice Street for the ground.

DUNFERMLINE ATHLETIC FC

Founded: 1885 (**Entered League**: 1921)
Nickname: 'The Pars'
Ground: East End Park, Halbeath Road, Dunfermline, Fife, KY12 7RB
Ground Capacity: 11,780 (All seats)
Record Attendance: 27,816 (30th April 1968)
Pitch Size: 115 × 71 yards

Colours: Black and White Striped shirts, White shorts
Telephone Nº: (01383) 724295
Ticket Office: (01383) 745909
Fax Number: (01383) 741098
Web Site: www.dafc.co.uk
E-mail: enquiries@dafc.co.uk

GENERAL INFORMATION

Car Parking: Limited spaces in a Car Park at the ground.
Coach Parking: Leys Park Road
Nearest Railway Station: Dunfermline Queen Margaret (10 minutes walk)
Nearest Bus Station: Queen Anne Street, Dunfermline (10 minutes walk)
Club Shop: At the Ground
Opening Times: Tuesday to Friday 10.00am – 4.00pm and Saturday Matchdays 10.00am–12.00pm and 5.00pm–5.30pm
Telephone Nº: (01383) 724295

GROUND INFORMATION

Away Supporters' Entrances & Sections:
Turnstiles 10-15 for the East Stand. Turnstiles 16-18 for the North East Stand

ADMISSION INFO (2017/2018 PRICES)

Adult Seating: £18.00 – £20.00
Under-18s/Other Concessions Seating: £12.00 – £14.00
Under-12s Seating: £5.00
Programme Price: £3.00

DISABLED INFORMATION

Wheelchairs: 12 spaces each for home & away fans
Helpers: One admitted per wheelchair
Prices: Concessionary prices for the wheelchair disabled. Helpers are admitted free of charge
Disabled Toilets: Available in West and East Stands and also in the Main Stand Hospitality Area
Contact: (01383) 745909 (Bookings are necessary – Away fans contact Matthew Ford)

Travelling Supporters' Information:
Routes: From the Forth Road Bridge and Perth: Exit the M90 at Junction 3 and take the A907 (Halbeath Road) into Dunfermline – the ground is on right; From Kincardine Bridge and Alloa: Take the A985 to the A994 into Dunfermline. Take Pittencrief Street, Glen Bridge and Carnegie Drive to Sinclair Gardens roundabout. Take the 1st exit toward the Traffic Lights then turn right into Ley's Park Road. Take the second exit on the right into the Car Park at the rear of the stadium.

EAST FIFE FC

Founded: 1903 (**Entered League**: 1903)
Nickname: 'The Fife'
Ground: Bayview Stadium, Harbour View, Methil, Fife   KY8 3RW
Ground Capacity: 2,000 (All seats)
Record Attendance: 22,515 (2nd January 1950)
Pitch Size: 110 × 70 yards

Colours: Gold and Black shirts with White shorts
Telephone Nº: (01333) 426323
Ticket Office: (01333) 426323
Web Site: www.eastfifefc.info
E-mail: office@eastfifefc.info

GENERAL INFORMATION

Car Parking: Adjacent to the ground
Coach Parking: Adjacent to the ground
Nearest Railway Station: Kirkcaldy (8 miles)
Nearest Bus Station: Leven
Club Shop: At the ground
Opening Times: Matchdays and normal office hours
Telephone Nº: (01333) 426323

GROUND INFORMATION

Away Supporters' Entrances & Sections:
Accommodated within the Main Stand

ADMISSION INFO (2017/2018 PRICES)

Adult Seating: £15.00
Child Seating: £5.00
Concessionary Seating: £12.00
Note: Family tickets are also available
Programme Price: £2.00

DISABLED INFORMATION

Wheelchairs: 24 spaces available in total
Helpers: Admitted
Prices: Normal prices charged for the disabled and helpers
Disabled Toilets: Yes
Contact: (01333) 426323 (Bookings are necessary)

Travelling Supporters' Information:
Routes: Take the A915 from Kirkcaldy past Buckhaven and Methil to Leven. Turn right at the traffic lights and go straight on at the first roundabout then turn right at the second roundabout. Cross Bawbee Bridge and turn left at the next roundabout. The ground is the first turning on the left after ¼ mile.

EDINBURGH CITY FC

Founded: 1928 (re-formed 1986)
Nickname: 'The Citizens'
Ground: Ainslie Park, 94 Pilton Drive, Edinburgh, EH5 2HF
Ground Capacity: 3,500
Seating Capacity: 504
Record Attendance: 5,740 (1936)

Pitch Size: 109 × 72 yards
Colours: White shirts with Black shorts
Contact Address: Jim Lumsden, 74 Lochend Road South, Edinburgh EH7 6DR
Telephone Nº: 07709 564141
Web Site: www.edinburghcityfc.com

GENERAL INFORMATION

Social Club: 74 Lochend Road South, Edinburgh EH7 6DR
Telephone Nº: 0845 463-1932
Car Parking: At the ground
Coach Parking: At the ground by prior arrangement
Nearest Railway Station: Edinburgh Haymarket (2¾ miles)
Nearest Bus Station: St. Andrew's Square
Club Shop: At the ground on matchdays only or: www.thefootballnation.co.uk/edinburgh-city-fc-online-store
Opening Times: Monday to Saturday 9.00am to 5.00pm.
Telephone Nº: (0131) 228-8614

GROUND INFORMATION

Away Supporters' Entrances & Sections:
No usual segregation

ADMISSION INFO (2017/2018 PRICES)

Adult Standing/Seating: £12.00
Child Standing/Seating: £6.00
Concessionary Standing/Seating: £6.00
Programme Price: £2.00

DISABLED INFORMATION

Wheelchairs: Accommodated
Helpers: Admitted
Prices: Concessionary prices apply for fans with disabilities
Disabled Toilets: Available
Contact: (0131) 552-7854   (Bookings are not necessary)

Travelling Supporters' Information:
Routes: From the West: Take the A90 Queensferry Road into Edinburgh and continue until reaching the A902 (Telford Road). Turn left into Telford Road and take the 3rd exit at the roundabout into Ferry Road. Turn left into Pilton Road immediately after passing the Morrisons Supermarket and enter the ground through Ainslie Park leisure centre; From the East: Take the A1 into Edinburgh and at the 1st roundabout take the 2nd exit into Milton Link. At the next roundabout (¼ mile) take the 2nd exit onto Sir Harry Lauder Road (A199). Continue along the A199 for approximately 2½ miles past Leith then turn left onto the A902 which continues into Ferry Road. Turn into Pilton Road just before the Morrisons Supermarket, then as above.

ELGIN CITY FC

Founded: 1893   (**Entered League**: 2000)
Nickname: 'Black and Whites'
Ground: Borough Briggs, Borough Briggs Road, Elgin   IV30 1AP
Ground Capacity: 4,520
Seating Capacity: 480
Record Attendance: 12,640 (17th February 1968)

Pitch Size: 120 × 86 yards
Colours: Black and White Striped shirts, Black shorts
Telephone Nº: (01343) 551114
Ticket Information: (01343) 551114
Fax Number: (01343) 547921
Web Site: www.elgincity.co.uk
E-mail: elgincityfc@btconnect.com

GENERAL INFORMATION

Car Parking: Lossie Green Car Park (2 minutes walk)
Coach Parking: Lossie Green Car Park (2 minutes walk)
Nearest Railway Station: Elgin (1 mile)
Nearest Bus Station: Elgin (¼ mile)
Club Shop: At the ground
Opening Times: Weekdays 9.30am to 4.30pm and also Saturdays 12.30am to 5.00pm (home matchdays only)
Telephone Nº: (01343) 551114

GROUND INFORMATION

Away Supporters' Entrances & Sections:
West End entrances for the Covered Enclosure

ADMISSION INFO (2017/2018 PRICES)

Adult Standing: £12.00
Adult Seating: £14.00
Child/Senior Citizen Standing: £7.00
Child/Senior Citizen Seating: £9.00
Programme Price: £2.00

DISABLED INFORMATION

Wheelchairs: Accommodated
Helpers: Admitted
Prices: Please contact the club for details
Disabled Toilets: Available
Contact: (01343) 551114   (Bookings are not necessary)

Travelling Supporters' Information:
Routes: Take the Alexandra bypass to the roundabout ½ mile from the City Centre and turn left towards Lossiemouth. Borough Briggs Road is on the left.

FALKIRK FC

Founded: 1876 (**Entered League**: 1902)
Nickname: 'The Bairns'
Ground: The Falkirk Stadium, 4 Stadium Way, Falkirk   FK2 9EE
Ground Capacity: 8,003 (All seats)
Pitch Size: 112 x 75 yards

Colours: Navy Blue shirts with White shorts
Telephone Nº: (01324) 624121
Ticket Office: (01324) 624121
Web Site: www.falkirkfc.co.uk
E-mail: feedback@falkirkfc.co.uk

GENERAL INFORMATION
Car Parking: A large Car Park is adjacent
Coach Parking: Available nearby
Nearest Railway Station: Falkirk Grahamston (1 mile)
Nearest Bus Station: Falkirk (1 mile)
Club Shop: At the stadium
Opening Times: 10.00am to 4.00pm
Telephone Nº: (01324) 624121

GROUND INFORMATION
Away Supporters' Entrances & Sections:
North Stand

ADMISSION INFO (2017/2018 PRICES)
Adult Seating: £18.00 – £20.00
Under-18s Seating: £6.00–£7.00 (Under-12s admitted free)
Concessionary Seating: £12.00 – £13.00
Note: Family Tickets are also available
Programme Price: £2.50

DISABLED INFORMATION
Wheelchairs: Accommodated
Helpers: Admitted
Prices: Free of charge for the disabled and helpers
Disabled Toilets: Available
Contact: (01324) 624121   (Bookings are necessary)

Travelling Supporters' Information:
Routes: Exit the M9 at Junction 6 and take the A904 towards Falkirk. Continue into Falkirk at the Westfield/Laurieston roundabout along Grangemouth Road and take the first right into Alexander Avenue. Then take the 2nd right into Westfield Street and the ground is on the right.

FORFAR ATHLETIC FC

Founded: 1885 (**Entered League**: 1921)
Nickname: 'Loons'
Ground: Station Park, Carseview Road, Forfar, Angus   DD8 3BT
Ground Capacity: 6,777   **Seating Capacity**: 739
Record Attendance: 10,780 (2nd February 1970)
Pitch Size: 113 × 70 yards

Colours: Shirts are Navy Blue with a Sky Blue shoulder panel, Navy Blue shorts
Telephone Nº: (01307) 463576
Ticket Office: (01307) 463576
Web Site: www.forfarathletic.co.uk

GENERAL INFORMATION

Car Parking: Market Muir Car Park and adjacent streets
Coach Parking: Market Muir Car Park
Nearest Railway Station: Dundee or Arbroath (14 miles)
Nearest Bus Station: Forfar (½ mile)
Club Shop: At the ground on Matchdays only

GROUND INFORMATION

Away Supporters' Entrances & Sections:
West End entrances for West End Terracing and North part of the Main Stand

ADMISSION INFO (2017/2018 PRICES)

Adult Standing: £12.00
Adult Seating: £13.00
Child/Senior Citizen Standing: £6.00
Child/Senior Citizen Seating: £7.00
Programme Price: £2.00

DISABLED INFORMATION

Wheelchairs: 4 spaces each for home and away fans accommodated to the west of the Main Stand
Helpers: Please phone the club for details
Prices: Please phone the club for details
Disabled Toilets: One available
Contact: (01307) 463576   (Bookings are necessary)

Travelling Supporters' Information:
Routes: Take the A85/M90 to Dundee and then the A929. Exit at the 2nd turn-off (signposted for Forfar). On the outskirts of Forfar, turn right at the T-junction and then left at the next major road. The ground is signposted on the left (down the cobbled street with the railway arch).

GREENOCK MORTON FC

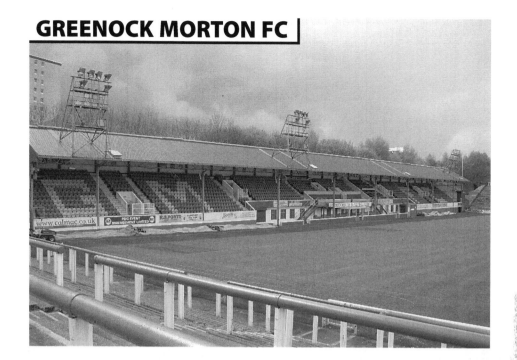

Founded: 1874 (**Entered League**: 1893)
Nickname: 'Ton'
Ground: Cappielow Park, Sinclair Street, Greenock, PA15 2TY
Ground Capacity: 11,589 **Seating Capacity**: 6,039
Record Attendance: 23,500 (29th April 1921)

Pitch Size: 110 × 71 yards
Colours: Blue and White hooped shirts, White shorts
Telephone/Ticket Office N°: (01475) 723571
Web Site: www.gmfc.net
E-mail: antonia@gmfc.net

GENERAL INFORMATION

Car Parking: At the ground (£3.00 fee) or Street parking
Coach Parking: James Watt Dock
Nearest Railway Station: Cartsdyke (½ mile)
Nearest Bus Station: Town Centre (1½ miles)
Club Shop: Within "Smiths of Greenock", West Blackhall Street, Greenock. There is also a Merchandise Unit in Sinclair Street, outside of the ground open matchdays only.
Opening Times: Monday to Friday 9.00am to 4.00pm
Telephone N°: (01475) 888555 **Fax N°**: (01475) 781084
Club Shop Web Site: www.themortonshop.com

GROUND INFORMATION

Away Supporters' Entrances & Sections:
Match dependent – please check the web site for details

ADMISSION INFO (2017/2018 PRICES)

Adult Standing and Seating: £20.00 (£18.00 in advance)
Concessionary Standing: £15.00 (purchased in advance)
Ages 12 to 16: £5.00 (purchased in advance)
Note: Under-12s are admitted free of charge when accompanied by a paying adult.
Programme Price: £3.00

DISABLED INFORMATION

Wheelchairs: 5 spaces each for home and away fans accommodated below the Grandstand
Helpers: One helper admitted per disabled fan
Prices: £15.00 for the disabled, free of charge for helpers
Disabled Toilets: One available
Contact: (01475) 723571 (Bookings are necessary)

Travelling Supporters' Information:
Routes: From the North: Take the M8 to the A8. From Port Glasgow follow the A78 to Greenock. Cappielow Park is on the left after passing under the railway bridge; From the South: Take the A78 to Greenock. Follow the road past IBM then turn right at the second set of lights into Dunlop Street. Follow this road until it turns sharp left and goes downhill and continue to the traffic lights facing the river. Turn right onto the A8, cross two roundabouts and Cappielow Park is on the right hand side of the road.

INVERNESS CALEDONIAN THISTLE FC

Founded: 1994 (**Entered League**: 1994)
Former Names: Caledonian Thistle FC
Nickname: 'The Jags' 'Caley'
Ground: Tulloch Caledonian Stadium, Stadium Road,
Inverness   IV1 1FF
Ground Capacity: 7,700 (all seats)
Record Attendance: 7,700

Colours: Shirts are Royal Blue and Red,
Shorts are Royal Blue
Telephone Nº: (01463) 222880 (Ground)
Ticket Office: (01463) 227451
Fax Number: (01463) 227479
Web Site: www.ictfc.co.uk

GENERAL INFORMATION
Car Parking: At the ground
Coach Parking: At the ground
Nearest Railway Station: Inverness (1 mile)
Nearest Bus Station: Inverness
Club Shop: At the ground
Opening Times: Weekdays and Matchdays 9.00am–4.30pm
Telephone Nº: (01463) 227451

GROUND INFORMATION
Away Supporters' Entrances & Sections:
South Stand

ADMISSION INFO (2017/2018 PRICES)
Adult Seating: £20.00 – £22.00
Under-16s Seating: £10.00
Senior Citizen/Ages 16 to 25 Seating: £15.00 – £17.00
Note: Prices vary depending on the category of the game.

DISABLED INFORMATION
Wheelchairs: 52 spaces available in total
Helpers: Admitted
Prices: Free of charge for the disabled and their helpers
Disabled Toilets: Available
Contact: (01463) 222880   (Bookings are necessary)

Travelling Supporters' Information:
Routes: The ground is adjacent to Kessock Bridge. From the South: Take the A9 to Inverness and turn right at the roundabout before the bridge over the Moray Firth; From the North: Take the A9 over the bridge and turn left at the roundabout for the ground.

LIVINGSTON FC

Founded: 1943 (**Entered League**: 1974)
Former Names: Ferranti Thistle FC, Meadowbank Thistle FC
Nickname: 'The Lions'
Ground: Tony Macaroni Arena, Alderstone Road, Livingston EH54 7DN
Ground Capacity: 10,006 (All seats)

Record Attendance: 10,006 (vs Rangers)
Pitch Size: 105 × 72 yards
Colours: Gold shirts with Black shorts
Telephone Nº: (01506) 417000
Web Site: www.livingstonfc.co.uk
E-mail: lfcreception@livingstonfc.co.uk

GENERAL INFORMATION
Car Parking: Car Park at the ground by arrangement
Coach Parking: At the ground
Nearest Railway Station: Livingston
Nearest Bus Station: Livingston
Club Shop: At the Stadium
Opening Times: Daily – please phone for further details

GROUND INFORMATION
Away Supporters' Entrances & Sections:
East Stand entrances and accommodation

ADMISSION INFO (2017/2018 PRICES)
Adult Seating: £18.00
Concessionary Seating: £10.00
Under-16s Seating: £5.00
Family Ticket: £46.00 (2 Adults + 2 Children under 16)
Programme Price: £2.50

DISABLED INFORMATION
Wheelchairs: Accommodated
Helpers: Admitted
Prices: Normal prices for fans with disabilities. Helpers free
Disabled Toilets: Available
Contact: (01506) 417000   (Bookings are necessary)

Travelling Supporters' Information:
Routes: Exit the M8 at the Livingston turn-off and take the A899 to the Cousland Interchange. Turn right into Cousland Road, pass the Hospital, then turn left into Alderstone Road and the stadium is on the left opposite the Campus.

MONTROSE FC

Founded: 1879 (**Entered League**: 1929)
Nickname: 'Gable Endies'
Ground: Links Park Stadium, Wellington Street, Montrose   DD10 8QD
Ground Capacity: 4,936
Seating Capacity: 1,338
Record Attendance: 8,983 (vs Dundee – 17/3/1973)

Pitch Size: 113 × 70 yards
Colours: Royal Blue shirts with Blue shorts
Telephone Nº: (01674) 673200
Ticket Office: (01674) 673200
Fax Number: (01674) 677311
Web Site: www.montrosefc.co.uk
E-mail: office@montrosefc.co.uk

GENERAL INFORMATION

Car Parking: At the ground and Street parking also
Coach Parking: Mid-Links
Nearest Railway Station: Montrose Western Road
Nearest Bus Station: High Street, Montrose
Club Shop: At the ground
Opening Times: Matchdays 10.00am to 3.00pm and also on Monday and Wednesday evenings
Telephone Nº: (01674) 673200

GROUND INFORMATION

Away Supporters' Entrances & Sections:
No usual segregation

ADMISSION INFO (2017/2018 PRICES)

Adult Standing: £13.00
Adult Seating: £13.00
Child/Senior Citizen Standing: £7.00
Child/Senior Citizen Seating: £7.00
Adult and Child Ticket: £16.00
Programme Price: £2.00

DISABLED INFORMATION

Wheelchairs: 5 spaces available in the Main Stand
Helpers: Please phone the club for information
Prices: Please phone the club for information
Disabled Toilets: 2 available in the Main Stand
Contact: (01674) 673200 (Bookings are helpful)

Travelling Supporters' Information:
Routes: Take the main A92 Coastal Road to Montrose. Once in the town, the ground is well signposted and is situated in the Mid-Links area.

PETERHEAD FC

Founded: 1891 (**Entered League**: 2000)
Nickname: 'Blue Toon'
Ground: Balmoor Stadium, Peterhead   AB42 1EQ
Ground Capacity: 3,150
Seating Capacity: 980
Record Attendance: 4,855
Pitch Size: 110 × 70 yards

Colours: Royal Blue Shirts with Sky Blue sleeves,
Shorts are Royal Blue with White piping
Telephone Nº: (01779) 478256
Fax Number: (01779) 490682
Web Site: www.peterheadfc.co.uk
E-mail: office@peterheadfc.co.uk

GENERAL INFORMATION

Car Parking: At the ground
Coach Parking: At the ground
Nearest Railway Station: Aberdeen
Nearest Bus Station: Peterhead
Club Shop: At the ground
Opening Times: Monday to Saturday 9.00am to 5.00pm
Telephone Nº: (01779) 478256

GROUND INFORMATION

Away Supporters' Entrances & Sections:
Segregation only used when required which is very rare

ADMISSION INFO (2017/2018 PRICES)

Adult Standing: £12.00
Adult Seating: £14.00
Child/Concessionary Standing: £6.00
Child/Concessionary Seating: £8.00
Programme Price: £2.50

DISABLED INFORMATION

Wheelchairs: Accommodated
Helpers: Please phone the club for details
Prices: Please phone the club for details
Disabled Toilets: Available
Contact: (01779) 473434   (Bookings are necessary)

Travelling Supporters' Information:
Routes: The ground is situated on the left of the main road from Fraserburgh (A952), 300 yards past the swimming pool.

QUEEN OF THE SOUTH FC

Founded: 1919 (**Entered League**: 1923)
Nickname: 'The Doonhamers'
Ground: Palmerston Park, Terregles Street, Dumfries, DG2 9BA
Ground Capacity: 8,690
Seating Capacity: 3,377
Record Attendance: 26,552 (23rd February 1952)

Pitch Size: 115 × 70 yards
Colours: Blue shirts and shorts
Telephone Nº: (01387) 254853
Ticket Office: (01387) 254853
Fax Number: (01387) 240470
Web Site: www.qosfc.com
E-mail: admin@qosfc.com

GENERAL INFORMATION
Car Parking: Car Park adjacent to the ground
Coach Parking: Car Park adjacent to the ground
Nearest Railway Station: Dumfries (¾ mile)
Nearest Bus Station: Dumfries Whitesands (5 minutes walk)
Club Shop: At the ground
Opening Times: Weekdays 9.00am to 4.00pm and Saturday Matchdays 11.30am to 5.00pm
Telephone Nº: (01387) 254853

GROUND INFORMATION
Away Supporters' Entrances & Sections:
Terregles Street entrances for the East Stand

ADMISSION INFO (2017/2018 PRICES)
Adult Standing: £16.00   **Adult Seating**: £16.00
Senior Citizen Standing/Seating: £9.00
Under-16s Standing/Seating: £5.00
Programme Price: £2.50

DISABLED INFORMATION
Wheelchairs: Accommodated in front of the East Stand
Prices: Free of charge for helpers. Prices for the disabled depend on the age of the supporter.
Disabled Toilets: Available
Contact: (01387) 254853   (Bookings are not necessary except for games against Rangers FC)

Travelling Supporters' Information:
Routes: From the East: Take the A75 to Dumfries and follow the ring road over the River Nith. Turn left at the 1st roundabout then right at the 2nd roundabout (the Kilmarnock/Glasgow Road roundabout). The ground is a short way along past the Tesco store; From the West: Take the A75 to Dumfries and proceed along ring road to the 1st roundabout (Kilmarnock/Glasgow Road) then as from the East; From the North: Take A76 to Dumfries and carry straight across 1st roundabout for the ground.

QUEEN'S PARK FC   (HAMPDEN PARK)

Founded: 1867   (**Entered League**: 1900)
Nickname: 'The Spiders'
Ground: Hampden Park, Mount Florida, Glasgow, G42 9BA
Ground Capacity: 52,000 (All seats)
Record Attendance: 150,239 (17th April 1937)

Pitch Size: 115 × 75 yards
Colours: Black and White hooped shirts, White shorts
Telephone/Ticket Office Nº: (0141) 632-1275
Fax Number: (0141) 636-1612
Web Site: www.queensparkfc.co.uk
E-mail: secretary@queensparkfc.co.uk

GENERAL INFORMATION
Car Parking: Car park at the Stadium
Coach Parking: Car park at the Stadium
Nearest Railway Station: Mount Florida and King's Park (both 5 minutes walk)
Nearest Bus Station: Buchanan Street
Club Shop: At the ground
Opening Times: During home matches only
Telephone Nº: (0141) 632-1275

GROUND INFORMATION
Away Supporters' Entrances & Sections: South Stand

ADMISSION INFO (2017/2018 PRICES)
Adult Seating: £14.00
Senior Citizen Seating: £5.00
Concessionary Seating: £3.00 (includes the unemployed)
Note: Only the South Stand is presently used for games

DISABLED INFORMATION
Wheelchairs: 160 spaces available in total
Helpers: Admitted
Prices: Free for the disabled. Helpers normal prices
Disabled Toilets: Available
Contact: (0141) 632-1275   (Bookings are necessary)

Travelling Supporters' Information:
Routes: From the South: Take the A724 to the Cambuslang Road and at Eastfield branch left into Main Street and follow through Burnhill Street and Westmuir Place into Prospecthill Road. Turn left into Aikenhead Road and right into Mount Annan for Kinghorn Drive and the Stadium; From the South: Take the A77 Fenwick Road, through Kilmarnock Road into Pollokshaws Road then turn right into Langside Avenue. Pass through Battle Place to Battlefield Road and turn left into Cathcart Road. Turn right into Letherby Drive, right into Carmunnock Road and 1st left into Mount Annan Drive for the Stadium; From the North & East: Exit M8 Junction 15 and passing Infirmary on left proceed into High Street and cross the Albert Bridge into Crown Street. Join Cathcart Road and proceed South until it becomes Carmunnock Road. Turn left into Mount Annan Drive and left again into Kinghorn Drive for the Stadium.

RAITH ROVERS FC

Founded: 1883 (**Entered League**: 1902)
Nickname: 'The Rovers'
Ground: Stark's Park, Pratt Street, Kirkcaldy, KY1 1SA
Ground Capacity: 10,104 (All seats)
Record Attendance: 31,306 (7th February 1953)
Pitch Size: 113 × 70 yards

Colours: Navy Blue shirts with White shorts
Telephone Nº: (01592) 263514
Ticket Office: (01592) 263514
Fax Number: (01592) 642833
Web Site: www.raithrovers.net
E-mail: info@raithrovers.net

GENERAL INFORMATION

Car Parking: Esplanade and Beveridge Car Park
Coach Parking: Railway Station & Esplanade
Nearest Railway Station: Kirkcaldy (15 minutes walk)
Nearest Bus Station: Kirkcaldy (15 minutes walk)
Club Shop: ACA Sports, High Street, Kirkcaldy
Opening Times: Monday to Saturday 9.00am to 5.00pm
Telephone Nº: (01592) 263514

GROUND INFORMATION

Away Supporters' Entrances & Sections:
North Stand

ADMISSION INFO (2017/2018 PRICES)

Adult Seating: £15.00
Senior Citizen/Child Seating: £8.00
Note: One adult and one child are admitted for £21.00
Programme Price: £2.00

DISABLED INFORMATION

Wheelchairs: 12 spaces each for home and away fans accommodated in the North & South Stands
Helpers: One helper admitted per wheelchair
Prices: Free of charge for the helpers. Disabled pay concessionary prices
Disabled Toilets: Available in the North and South Stands
Are Bookings Necessary: Only for all-ticket games
Contact: (01592) 263514

Travelling Supporters' Information:
Routes: Take the M8 to the end then follow the A90/M90 over the Forth Road Bridge. Exit the M90 at Junction 1 and follow the A921 to Kirkcaldy. On the outskirts of town, turn left at the B & Q roundabout from which the floodlights can be seen. The ground is raised on the hill nearby.

STENHOUSEMUIR FC

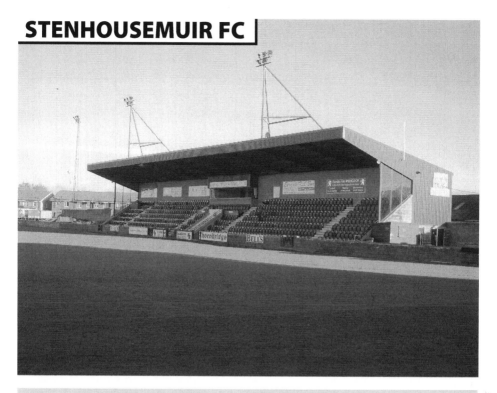

Founded: 1884 **(Entered League**: 1921)
Former Names: Heather Rangers FC
Nickname: 'Warriors'
Ground: Ochilview Park, Gladstone Road, Stenhousemuir FK5 4QL
Ground Capacity: 3,096 **Seating Capacity**: 626
Record Attendance: 12,500 (11th March 1950)

Pitch Size: 110 × 72 yards
Colours: Maroon shirts with White shorts
Telephone Nº: (01324) 562992
Fax Number: (01324) 562980
Web Site: www.stenhousemuirfc.com
E-mail: info@stenhousemuirfc.com

GENERAL INFORMATION
Car Parking: Street parking only
Coach Parking: Tryst Showground (adjacent)
Nearest Railway Station: Larbert (1 mile)
Nearest Bus Station: Falkirk (2½ miles)
Club Shop: At the ground
Opening Times: Weekdays from 9.00am to 5.00pm (closed on Wednesday afternoons) and from 2.00pm on Saturday matchdays
Telephone Nº: (01324) 562992

GROUND INFORMATION
Away Supporters' Entrances & Sections:
Terracing entrances and accommodation

ADMISSION INFO (2017/2018 PRICES)
Adult Standing: £12.00 – £18.00
Adult Seating: £13.00 – £18.00
Senior Citizen/Concessionary Standing: £7.00 – £10.00
Senior Citizen/Concessionary Seating: £8.00 – £10.00
Note: Prices vary depending on the category of the game

DISABLED INFORMATION
Wheelchairs: Accommodated
Helpers: Admitted
Prices: Free of charge for disabled fans
Disabled Toilets: Available in the Gladstone Road Stand
Contact: (01324) 562992 (Bookings are not necessary)

Travelling Supporters' Information:
Routes: Exit the M876 at Junction 2 and follow signs for Stenhousemuir. Pass the Old Hospital and turn right after the Golf Course. The ground is on the left behind the houses – the floodlights are visible for ¼ mile.

STIRLING ALBION FC

Founded: 1945 (**Entered League**: 1946)
Nickname: 'The Binos'
Ground: Forth Bank Stadium, Springkerse, Stirling, FK7 7UJ
Ground Capacity: 3,808
Seating Capacity: 2,508
Record Attendance: 3,808 (17th February 1996)

Pitch Size: 110 × 74 yards
Colours: Shirts are Red with White sleeves, Red Shorts
Telephone Nº: (01786) 450399
Ticket Office: (01786) 450399
Fax Number: (01786) 448592
Web site: www.stirlingalbionfc.co.uk
E-mail: office@stirlingalbionfc.co.uk

GENERAL INFORMATION

Car Parking: At the ground
Coach Parking: Adjacent to the ground
Nearest Railway Station: Stirling (2 miles)
Nearest Bus Station: Stirling (2 miles)
Club Shop: At the ground
Opening Times: Weekdays and Matchdays from 10.00am to 4.00pm
Telephone Nº: (01786) 450399

GROUND INFORMATION

Away Supporters' Entrances & Sections:
South Terracing and East Stand

ADMISSION INFO (2017/2018 PRICES)

Adult Standing/Seating: £13.00
Concessionary Standing/Seating: £9.00
Under-16s Standing/Seating: £5.00
Note: Under-12s are admitted free of charge when accompanied by a paying adult.
Programme Price: £2.00

DISABLED INFORMATION

Wheelchairs: 18 spaces each for home and away fans
Helpers: Admitted
Prices: Free of charge for the disabled and helpers
Disabled Toilets: 2 available beneath each stand
Contact: (01786) 450399 (Bookings are necessary)

Travelling Supporters' Information:
Routes: Follow signs for Stirling from the M9/M80 Northbound. From Pirnhall Roundabout follow signs for Alloa/St. Andrew's to the 4th roundabout and then turn left for the stadium.

ST. MIRREN FC

Founded: 1877 (**Entered League**: 1890)
Nickname: 'The Saints' 'The Buddies'
Ground: The Paisley 2021 Stadium, St. Mirren Park, Greenhill Road, Paisley PA3 1RU
Ground Capacity: 8,023 (all seats)
Record Attendance: 47,428 (7th March 1925 – at former stadium in Love Street)
Pitch Size: 115 × 74 yards (105 × 68 metres)

Colours: Black and White striped shirts, Black shorts
Telephone N°: (0141) 889-2558
Ticket Line N°: (0141) 840-6130
Fax Number: (0141) 848-6444
Main Web Site: www.saintmirren.net
Ticketing Web Site: www.smfctickets.co.uk
E-mail: info@saintmirren.net

GENERAL INFORMATION

Car Parking: Street parking plus limited parking in the Stadium car park
Coach Parking: Clark Street
Nearest Railway Station: Paisley St. James (400 yards) or Paisley Gilmour Street (10 minutes walk)
Nearest Bus Station: Paisley
Club Shop: At the stadium
Opening Times: Daily from 10.00am to 2.00pm
Telephone N°: (0141) 840-6130

GROUND INFORMATION

Away Supporters' Entrances & Sections:
North Stand (N1-N5), turnstiles 17-20

ADMISSION INFO (2017/2018 PRICES)

Adult Seating: £20.00 – £22.00
Concessionary Seating: £10.00 – £12.00
Under-18s Seating: £5.00 – £12.00
Under-12s Seating: £2.00 – £5.00
Programme Price: £3.00

DISABLED INFORMATION

Wheelchairs: Accommodated in all Stands
Helpers: Admitted
Prices: £10.00 for each disabled fan and one helper (proof of entitlement may be required)
Disabled Toilets: Available in all the stands
Contact: (0141) 840-6130 (Bookings are necessary)

Travelling Supporters' Information:
Routes: From All Parts: Exit the M8 at Junction 29 and take the A726, keeping in the middle lane to avoid the A727 which is signposted for Irvine. At the St. James interchange, turn left onto the dual carriageway (Greenock Road) which has football pitches on the left. After the sharp bend, take the first turn on the right into Clark Street and, at the T-junction, turn left past the railway station into Greenhill Road. The stadium is on the right-hand side of the road.

STRANRAER FC

Founded: 1870 (**Entered League**: 1955)
Nickname: 'The Blues'
Ground: Stair Park, London Road, Stranraer, DG9 8BS
Ground Capacity: 4,178
Seating Capacity: 2,200
Record Attendance: 6,500 (24th January 1948)

Pitch Size: 112 × 70 yards
Colours: Blue shirts with White shorts
Telephone Nº: (01776) 703271
Ticket Office: (01776) 703271
Web Site: www.stranraerfc.org
E-mail: secretary@stranraerfc.org

GENERAL INFORMATION

Car Parking: Car Park at the ground
Coach Parking: Port Rodie, Stranraer
Nearest Railway Station: Stranraer (1 mile)
Nearest Bus Station: Port Rodie, Stranraer
Club Shop: At the ground
Opening Times: 2.15pm to 3.00pm and during half-time on Matchdays only
Telephone Nº: None

GROUND INFORMATION

Away Supporters' Entrances & Sections:
London Road entrances for the Visitors Stand

ADMISSION INFO (2017/2018 PRICES)

Adult Standing: £15.00
Adult Seating: £15.00
Under-16s Standing: £5.00
Under-16s Seating: £5.00
Concessionary Standing: £10.00
Concessionary Seating: £10.00
Programme Price: £2.00

DISABLED INFORMATION

Wheelchairs: 6 spaces each for Home and Away fans in front of the North Stand and South Stand
Helpers: Please phone the club for details
Prices: Please phone the club for details
Disabled Toilets: One in the North and South Stands
Contact: (01776) 703271 (Bookings are necessary)

Travelling Supporters' Information:
Routes: From the West: Take the A75 to Stranraer and the ground is on the left-hand side of the road in a public park shortly after entering the town; From the North: Take the A77 and follow it to where it joins with the A75 (then as West). The ground is set back from the road and the floodlights are clearly visible.

THE HIGHLAND FOOTBALL LEAGUE

Founded   1893

Secretary   Mr Rod Houston

Web site   www.highlandfootballleague.com

Clubs for the 2017/2018 Season

Brora Rangers FC .... Page 48

Buckie Thistle FC... Page 49

Clachnacuddin FC .... Page 50

Cove Rangers FC .... Page 51

Deveronvale FC .... Page 52

Formartine United FC .... Page 53

Forres Mechanics FC .... Page 54

Fort William FC .... Page 55

Fraserburgh FC .... Page 56

Huntly FC .... Page 57

Inverurie Loco Works FC .... Page 58

Keith FC .... Page 59

Lossiemouth FC.. Page 60

Nairn County FC .... Page 61

Rothes FC .... Page 62

Strathspey Thistle FC .... Page 63

Turriff United FC.. Page 64

Wick Academy FC .... Page 65

BRORA RANGERS FC

Founded: 1878
Nickname: 'The Cattachs'
Ground: Dudgeon Park Road, Brora   KW9 6QH
Ground Capacity: 4,000
Seating Capacity: 250
Record Attendance: 2,000 (31st August 1963)
Web site: brorarangers.football

Colours: Red shirts with White shorts
Telephone/Fax Nº: (01408) 621231
Social Club Phone Nº: (01408) 621570
Contact Phone Nº: (01408) 621114
Correspondence Address: Kevin Mackay,
2 Muirfield Road, Brora   KW9 6QP

GENERAL INFORMATION
Car Parking: Adjacent to the ground
Coach Parking: Adjacent to the ground
Nearest Railway Station: Brora
Nearest Bus Station: Brora
Club Shop: At the ground
Opening Times: Matchdays only
Telephone Nº: (01408) 621231

GROUND INFORMATION
Away Supporters' Entrances & Sections:
No usual segregation

ADMISSION INFO (2017/2018 PRICES)
Adult Standing: £9.00
Adult Seating: £9.00
Concessionary Standing: £5.00
Concessionary Seating: £5.00
Note: Under-14s are admitted free with a paying adult
Programme Price: £1.00

DISABLED INFORMATION
Wheelchairs: Accommodated
Helpers: Please phone the club for details
Prices: Please phone the club for details
Disabled Toilets: None at present (under construction)
Contact: (01408) 621231   (Bookings are necessary)

Travelling Supporters' Information:
Routes: Take the A9 Northbound from Inverness and the Stadium is situated on the right upon entering the town. It is clearly visible from the road.

BUCKIE THISTLE FC

Founded: 1889
Former Names: None
Nickname: 'The Jags'
Ground: New Victoria Park, Midmar Street, Buckie, AB56 1BJ
Pitch Size: 109 × 73 yards
Record Attendance: 8,168 (1st March 1958)

Ground Capacity: 5,000
Seating Capacity: 400
Colours: Green and White hooped shirts, White shorts
Correspondence: c/o David Pirie, St. Aethans, 33 Station Road, Findochty, AB56 4PJ
Telephone Nº: (01542) 831454
Web Site: www.buckiethistle.org

GENERAL INFORMATION
Car Parking: Adjacent to the ground
Coach Parking: Adjacent to the ground
Nearest Railway Station: Keith (12 miles)
Nearest Bus Station: Buckie
Club Shop: In the Supporters' Club inside the ground
Social Club: Victoria Park Function Hall at the ground
Social Club Telephone Nº: (01542) 831454

GROUND INFORMATION
Away Supporters' Entrances & Sections:
No usual segregation

ADMISSION INFO (2017/2018 PRICES)
Adult Standing: £8.00
Adult Seating: £8.00
Concessionary Standing/Seating: £4.00
Note: Under-14s are admitted free with a paying adult
Programme Price: £2.00

DISABLED INFORMATION
Wheelchairs: Accommodated in front of the stand
Helpers: Admitted
Prices: Normal prices apply
Disabled Toilets: Available in the Victoria Park Function Hall
Contact: (01542) 831454   (Bookings are helpful)

Travelling Supporters' Information:
Routes: From the East and West: Exit the A98 onto the A942 towards Buckie. Go straight on at the roundabout and travel along Buckie High Street. Turn left at the roundabout next to Cluny Square into West Church Street then take the 1st left into South Pringle Street. The ground is straight ahead.

CLACHNACUDDIN FC

Founded: 1886
Nickname: 'Lilywhites'
Ground: Grant Street Park, Wyvis Place, Inverness, IV3 6DR
Ground Capacity: 1,500
Seating Capacity: 154
Record Attendance: 9,000 (27th August 1951)
Pitch Size: 108 × 70 yards

Colours: White shirts with Black shorts
Telephone N°: (01463) 718261
Fax Number: (01463) 718261
Contact Address: Douglas Noble, 21 Leachkin Avenue, Inverness   IV3 8LH
Contact Phone N°: 07707 599966
Web site: clachfc.com

GENERAL INFORMATION

Car Parking: Adjacent to the ground
Coach Parking: Adjacent to the ground
Nearest Railway Station: Inverness
Nearest Bus Station: Inverness
Club Shop: At the ground
Opening Times: Matchdays only
Telephone N°: (01463) 718261

GROUND INFORMATION

Away Supporters' Entrances & Sections:
No usual segregation

ADMISSION INFO (2017/2018 PRICES)

Adult Standing: £8.00
Adult Seating: £9.00
Child Standing: £4.00
Child Seating: £5.00
Note: Under-14s are admitted free with a paying adult

DISABLED INFORMATION

Wheelchairs: Accommodated
Helpers: Admitted
Prices: Normal prices apply
Disabled Toilets: Available
Contact: (01463) 224706   (Bookings are not necessary)

Travelling Supporters' Information:
Routes: From the East and South: From the roundabout at the junction of the A9 and A96, proceed into the Town Centre and over the River Ness. Turn right at the traffic lights (onto the A862 to Dingwall), go up Kenneth Street and over the roundabout onto Telford Street for 200 yards before turning right into Telford Road opposite the Fish Shop. At the top, turn left onto Lower Kessack Street and left again. Finally, turn left into Wyvis Place and the ground is on the left.

COVE RANGERS FC

Following a decision to redevelop the site for residential use, Cove Rangers FC will not be playing home matches at Allan Park (pictured above) during the first half of the 2017/2018 season. The club are are currently working with Aberdeen City Council to build a new football stadium at Calder Park in Altens. Groundsharing agreements are in place with Inverurie Loco Works FC for the 2017/2018 season home fixtures so please contact the club for detailed venue information when the match schedule has been confirmed.

Founded: 1922
Nickname: None
Former Ground: Allan Park, Loriston Road, Cove, Aberdeen, AB12 3NR
Ground Capacity: 2,300
Seating Capacity: 200
Record Attendance: 2,300 (15th November 1992)
Pitch Size: 104 × 65 yards

Colours: Blue shirts and shorts
Telephone Nº: (01224) 896282
Fax Number: (01224) 896282
Contact Address: Duncan Little, 18 Lochinch Drive, Cove, Aberdeen AB12 3RY
Contact Phone Nº: 07710 648154 (Matchdays) or (01224) 896282 (Evenings)
Web Site: www.coverangersfc.com

GENERAL INFORMATION
Please contact the club for further information (see above).

GROUND INFORMATION
Please contact the club for further information (see above).

ADMISSION INFO (2017/2018 PRICES)
Adult Standing: £8.00
Adult Seating: £10.00
Child Standing: £4.00
Child Seating: £6.00
Note: Under-14s are admitted free with a paying adult
Programme Price: £1.50

DISABLED INFORMATION
Facilities available to disabled supporters will depend on the particular venue at which the 'home' game is to be played. Please contact the club for further information on the following contact number: (01224) 896282.

Travelling Supporters' Information:
Routes: Please contact the club for further information (see above).

DEVERONVALE FC

Founded: 1938
Nickname: 'The Vale'
Ground: Princess Royal Park, 56 Airlie Gardens, Banff AB45 1AZ
Ground Capacity: 2,651
Seating Capacity: 372
Record Attendance: 5,000 (27th April 1952)
Pitch Size: 109 × 78 yards

Colours: Shirts are Red with White trim, White shorts
Telephone Nº: (01261) 818303
Fax Number: (01261) 813753
Contact Address: Stewart McPherson, 8 Victoria Place, Banff AB45 1EL
Contact Phone Nº: (01261) 818303
Web Site: www.deveronvale.co.uk
E-mail: deveronvalefc@highlandleague.com

GENERAL INFORMATION

Car Parking: Adjacent to the ground plus street parking.
Coach Parking: Bridge Road Car Park
Nearest Railway Station: Keith (20 miles)
Nearest Bus Station: Macduff (1 mile)
Club Shop: At the ground
Opening Times: Matchdays only
Telephone Nº: (01261) 818303

GROUND INFORMATION

Away Supporters' Entrances & Sections:
No usual segregation

ADMISSION INFO (2017/2018 PRICES)

Adult Standing: £8.00
Adult Seating: £10.00
Child Standing: £4.00
Child Seating: £6.00
Note: Under-14s are admitted free with a paying adult

DISABLED INFORMATION

Wheelchairs: Accommodated
Helpers: Admitted
Prices: Please phone the club for details
Disabled Toilets: Available
Contact: (01261) 818303 (Bookings are necessary)

Travelling Supporters' Information:
Routes: From Aberdeen: Enter the town at Banff Bridge – the ground is situated ¼ mile along on the right; From Inverness: Travel through Banff on the main bypass and the ground is situated on the left, ¼ mile before Banff Bridge.

FORMARTINE UNITED FC

Founded: 1946
Nickname: 'United'
Ground: North Lodge Park, Pitmedden   AB41 7XA
Ground Capacity: 1,800
Seating Capacity: 300
Record Attendance: 1,500

Colours: Red & White striped shirts with White shorts
Telephone Nº: (01651) 843266 (Matchdays only)
Contact Address: Brian Braidwood, 27 Links Road
Bridge of Don, Aberdeen   AB23 8DD
Contact Phone Nº: 0781 507-2024
Web site: www.formartineunitedfc.co.uk

GENERAL INFORMATION
Car Parking: At the ground
Coach Parking: At the ground
Nearest Railway Station: Inverurie (11 miles)
Nearest Bus Station: Inverurie
Club Shop: At the ground
Opening Times: Matchdays only

GROUND INFORMATION
Away Supporters' Entrances & Sections:
No usual segregation

ADMISSION INFO (2017/2018 PRICES)
Adult Standing: £9.00
Adult Seating: £9.00
Concessionary Standing/Seating: £5.00
Under-12s Standing/Seating: £5.00
Programme Price: £2.00

DISABLED INFORMATION
Wheelchairs: Accommodated
Helpers: Admitted with prior notice
Prices: Normal prices apply for the disabled and helpers
Disabled Toilets: Available
Contact: 0781 507-2024

Travelling Supporters' Information:
Routes: Pitmedden is located approximately 15 miles north of Aberdeen on the A920 between Oldmeldrum and Ellon. North Lodge Park is situated just to the west of Pitmedden by the junction of the A920 and the B9000 which heads into Pitmedden itself.

FORRES MECHANICS FC

Founded: 1884
Nickname: 'Can Cans'
Ground: Mosset Park, Lea Road, Forres   IV36 1AU
Ground Capacity: 1,400
Seating Capacity: 502
Record Attendance: 7,000 (2nd February 1957)
Pitch Size: 106 × 69 yards

Colours: Maroon & Gold striped shirts, Maroon shorts
Telephone/Fax Number: (01309) 675096
Contact Address: David W. Macdonald, Secretary,
7 Brinuth Place, Elgin   IV30 6YW
Contact Phone Nº: (01343) 544294
Mobile Phone Contact Nº: 07779 782799
Web site: www.forresmechanics.net

GENERAL INFORMATION

Car Parking: At the ground
Coach Parking: At the ground
Nearest Railway Station: Forres
Nearest Bus Station: Forres
Club Shop: At the ground
Opening Times: Matchdays only
Telephone Nº: (01309) 675096

GROUND INFORMATION

Away Supporters' Entrances & Sections:
No usual segregation

ADMISSION INFO (2017/2018 PRICES)

Adult Standing: £8.00   **Adult Seating**: £10.00
Child/Senior Citizen Standing: £6.00
Child/Senior Citizen Seating: £8.00
Note: Under-14s are admitted free with a paying adult
Programme Price: £1.00

DISABLED INFORMATION

Wheelchairs: Accommodated
Helpers: Admitted
Prices: Normal prices apply
Disabled Toilets: One available
Contact: (01309) 675096   (Bookings are not necessary)

Travelling Supporters' Information:
Routes: From A96 East (Inverness): Turn off the A96 onto the B9011. Continue along this road and pass Tesco, turn left at the roundabout then immediately right into Invererne Road. Follow for about ½ mile then turn right across Lea Bridge then left for the ground; From A96 West (Aberdeen): Drive into Forres on the A96 passing the ground on your left. After a short distance, turn left onto the A940 (Market Street). Immediately before the roundabout turn left into Invererne Road. Then as above.

FORT WILLIAM FC

Founded: 1984
Nickname: 'The Fort'
Ground: Claggan Park, Achintee Road, Fort William, PH33 6TE
Ground Capacity: 4,000
Seating Capacity: 400
Record Attendance: 1,500 (4th January 1986)

Pitch Size: 102 × 80 yards
Colours: Yellow shirts with Black shorts
Telephone Nº: (01397) 698003
Contact Address: Marie McMillan, 25 Ardnevis Road, Claggan, Fort William   PH33 6QW
Contact Phone Nº: 0780 304-9571
Web site: www.fortwilliamfc.co.uk

GENERAL INFORMATION

Car Parking: At the ground
Coach Parking: At the ground
Nearest Railway Station: Fort William
Nearest Bus Station: Fort William
Club Shop: Sales via the club's web site

GROUND INFORMATION

Away Supporters' Entrances & Sections:
No usual segregation

ADMISSION INFO (2017/2018 PRICES)

Adult Standing: £7.00   **Adult Seating**: £7.00
Concessionary Standing/Seating: £3.50
Note: Under-14s are admitted free with a paying adult
Programme Price: No programme is produced

DISABLED INFORMATION

Wheelchairs: Accommodated in the stand
Helpers: Please phone the club for details
Prices: Concessionary prices apply for the disabled
Disabled Toilets: None at present
Contact: 07747 892661   (Bookings are not necessary)

Travelling Supporters' Information:
Routes: From the South: Approaching Fort William on the A82, proceed on the bypass of the Town Centre. After 2 roundabouts continue on Belford Road past the Railway Station on the left and the Swimming Baths on the right. After ½ mile and crossing over the River Nevis, take the first right into Claggan Road and the ground is ½ mile on the left; From Inverness: Take the A98 into Fort William before taking the 2nd left after the Shell petrol into Claggan Road. Take the 1st right before Spar signposted for the Ben Nevis Footpath. The ground is 1st left opposite the footbridge.   SatNav users please select PH33 6PR

FRASERBURGH FC

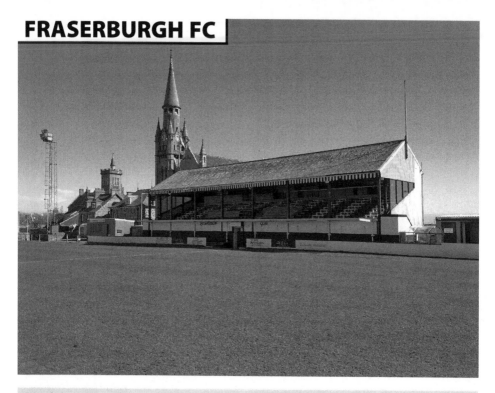

Founded: 1910
Nickname: 'The Broch'
Ground: Bellslea Park, Seaforth Street, Fraserburgh, AB43 9BB
Ground Capacity: 1,172
Seating Capacity: 300
Record Attendance: 5,800 (13th February 1954)
Pitch Size: 110 × 72 yards (101 × 60 metres)

Colours: Black and White striped shirts, Black shorts
Telephone Nº: (01346) 518444
Contact Address: Finlay Noble, 18 Bawdley Head, Fraserburgh AB43 9SE
Contact Phone Nº: (01346) 518444
Mobile Phone Contact Nº: 07852 178634
Web Site: www.fraserburghfc.scot
E-mail: finlay.noble@fraserburghfc.co.uk

GENERAL INFORMATION
Car Parking: At the ground
Coach Parking: At the ground
Nearest Railway Station: Aberdeen (40 miles)
Nearest Bus Station: Fraserburgh
Club Shop: Dick Sports, High Street, Fraserburgh
Opening Times: Monday to Friday 9.00am to 5.00pm and Saturday 9.00am to 1.00pm
Telephone Nº: (01346) 514120

GROUND INFORMATION
Away Supporters' Entrances & Sections:
No usual segregation

ADMISSION INFO (2017/2018 PRICES)
Adult Standing: £8.00
Adult Seating: £9.00
Child Standing: £4.00
Child Seating: £5.00
Note: Under-14s are admitted free with a paying adult
Programme Price: £2.00

DISABLED INFORMATION
Wheelchairs: Accommodated
Helpers: Admitted
Prices: Normal prices apply
Disabled Toilets: Available
Contact: (01346) 518444 (Bookings are not necessary)

Travelling Supporters' Information:
Routes: The ground is situated in the Town Centre, off Seaforth Street.

HUNTLY FC

Founded: 1928
Nickname: None
Ground: Christie Park, East Park Street, Huntly, Aberdeenshire AB54 8JE
Ground Capacity: 2,480
Seating Capacity: 270
Record Attendance: 4,500 (18th February 1995)
Pitch Size: 105 × 72 yards

Colours: Black and Gold shirts with Black shorts
Telephone Nº: (01466) 793548
Social Club Phone Nº: (01466) 793680
Contact Address: Alix Turner, 12 Forest Way, Huntly, AB54 8RG
Contact Phone Nº: (01466) 793548
Web Site: www.huntlyfc.co.uk
E-mail: huntlyfc@highlandleague.com

GENERAL INFORMATION
Car Parking: At the ground
Coach Parking: At the ground
Nearest Railway Station: Huntly (1 mile)
Nearest Bus Station: Huntly (¼ mile)
Club Shop: At the ground
Opening Times: Matchdays only

GROUND INFORMATION
Away Supporters' Entrances & Sections:
No usual segregation

ADMISSION INFO (2017/2018 PRICES)
Adult Standing: £8.00
Adult Seating: £9.00
Child/Concessionary Standing: £5.00
Child/Concessionary Seating: £6.00
Note: Two Under-14s are admitted free with a paying adult
Programme Price: £1.50

DISABLED INFORMATION
Wheelchairs: Accommodated
Helpers: Admitted at normal prices
Prices: Concessionary prices apply for the disabled
Disabled Toilets: Available
Contact: (01466) 793269 (Bookings are not necessary)

Travelling Supporters' Information:
Routes: Enter Town off the A96 and proceed along King George V Avenue and Gordon Street. Pass through the Town Centre Square, along Castle Street to East Park Street and the ground is on the right before the Castle.

INVERURIE LOCO WORKS FC

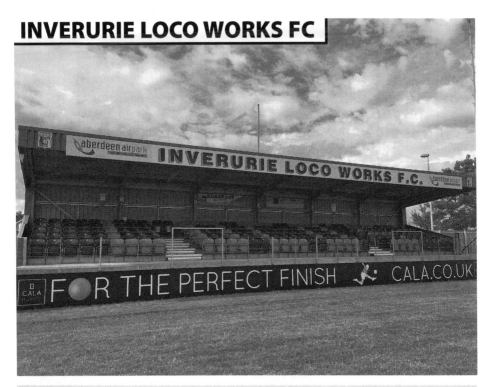

Founded: 1903
Nickname: 'Locos'
Ground: Harlaw Park, Harlaw Road, Inverurie, AB51 4SR
Ground Capacity: 2,500
Seating Capacity: 250
Record Attendance: 2,150
Pitch Size: 110 × 70 yards

Colours: Red and Black striped shirts, Black shorts
Telephone No: 07500 664434
Fax Number: (01467) 622168
Contact Address: Billy Thomson, 7 Birch Drive, Osprey Village, Inverurie AB51 6AN
Contact Phone No: 07500 664434
Web Site: www.inverurielocoworks.co.uk

GENERAL INFORMATION

Car Parking: At the ground
Coach Parking: At the ground
Nearest Railway Station: Inverurie
Nearest Bus Station: Inverurie
Club Shop: Merchandise available on matchdays and via inverurie-loco-works.footballkit.co.uk

GROUND INFORMATION

Away Supporters' Entrances & Sections:
No usual segregation

ADMISSION INFO (2017/2018 PRICES)

Adult Standing: £8.00   **Adult Seating**: £10.00
Child/Senior Citizen Standing: £4.00
Child/Senior Citizen Seating: £6.00
Note: Under-14s are admitted free with a paying adult
Programme Price: No programme is produced

DISABLED INFORMATION

Wheelchairs: Accommodated in the Covered Enclosure
Helpers: Admitted
Prices: Free of charge for the disabled
Disabled Toilets: Available
Contact: 07500 664434

Travelling Supporters' Information:
Routes: From the North: Take the A96 to the Inverurie bypass then turn left at the Morrisons roundabout along Blackhall Road and left at the next roundabout into Boroughmuir Drive. Cross the next roundabout and then turn 1st right into Hawlaw Road for the ground; From the South: Take the A96 to the Inverurie bypass then as above.

KEITH FC

Founded: 1910
Nickname: 'Maroons'
Ground: Kynoch Park, Balloch Road, Keith AB55 5EN
Ground Capacity: 4,000
Seating Capacity: 370
Record Attendance: 5,820 (4th February 1928)
Pitch Size: 110 × 75 yards

Colours: Shirts and shorts are Maroon with Blue trim
Telephone Nº: (01542) 882629
Fax Number: (01542) 882631
Contact Phone Nº: (01542) 882629
Web Site: www.keithfc.com
E-mail: keithfc@highlandleague.com

GENERAL INFORMATION

Car Parking: Street parking in Balloch Road, Moss Street and Reidhaven Square
Coach Parking: Balloch Road or Bridge Street Coach Park
Nearest Railway Station: Keith (1 mile)
Nearest Bus Station: Keith
Club Shop: At the ground
Opening Times: Wednesday to Friday 9.00am to 12.30pm
Telephone Nº: (01542) 882629

GROUND INFORMATION

Away Supporters' Entrances & Sections:
No usual segregation except for some Cup Ties

ADMISSION INFO (2017/2018 PRICES)

Adult Standing: £7.00
Adult Seating: £8.00
Child Standing: £4.00
Child Seating: £5.00
Note: Under-14s are admitted free with a paying adult
Programme Price: £1.00

DISABLED INFORMATION

Wheelchairs: Accommodated
Helpers: Admitted
Prices: Free entry for the disabled
Disabled Toilets: Available

Travelling Supporters' Information:
Routes: From Inverness: Follow the A96 through Keith before turning left opposite the newsagents and public toilets in Reidhaven Square. Follow signs for the Moray College Learning Centre, take the next left into Balloch Road and the ground is on the right; From Aberdeen: After Entering Keith turn right opposite the newsagents in Reidhaven Square. Then as above.

LOSSIEMOUTH FC

Founded: 1945
Nickname: 'Coasters'
Ground: Grant Park, Kellas Avenue, Lossiemouth IV31 6JG
Ground Capacity: 2,400 **Seating Capacity**: 150
Record Attendance: 2,800 (28th December 1948)
Pitch Size: 110 × 67 yards
Colours: Red shirts and shorts

Telephone Nº: (01343) 813717
Fax Number: (01343) 813717
Social Club Nº: (01343) 813168
Contact Address: Alan McIntosh, 3 Forties Place, Lossiemouth IV31 6SS
Contact Phone Nº: (01343) 813328 & (07890) 749053
Contact e-mail: alanlfcsec@aol.com
Web Site: www.lossiemouthfc.co.uk

GENERAL INFORMATION
Car Parking: At the ground
Coach Parking: At the ground
Nearest Railway Station: Elgin
Nearest Bus Station: Lossiemouth
Club Shop: At the ground
Opening Times: Matchdays only
Telephone Nº: (01343) 813168

GROUND INFORMATION
Away Supporters' Entrances & Sections:
No usual segregation

ADMISSION INFO (2017/2018 PRICES)
Adult Standing: £7.00 **Adult Seating**: £8.00
Child Standing: £3.50
Child Seating: £4.50
Note: Under-14s are admitted free with a paying adult
Programme Price: £1.00

DISABLED INFORMATION
Wheelchairs: Accommodated
Helpers: Admitted
Prices: Free of charge for the disabled
Disabled Toilets: Available
Contact: (01343) 813328 (Alan McIntosh) (Please book)

Travelling Supporters' Information:
Routes: Take the A941 to Lossiemouth. As you enter the town take the 3rd turning on the right into Moray Street. Continue along Moray Street then take the 4th turning on the right into Kellas Avenue. Grant Park is at the end of this road.

NAIRN COUNTY FC

Founded: 1914
Nickname: 'The Wee County'
Ground: Station Park, Balblair Road, Nairn IV12 5LT
Ground Capacity: 1,700
Seating Capacity: 250
Record Attendance: 4,000 (2nd September 1950)
Pitch Size: 106 × 70 yards

Colours: Yellow shirts with Black shorts
Telephone Nº: (01667) 454298
Fax Number: (01667) 456354
Contact Address: Donald Mathieson,
12 Duncan Drive, Nairn   IV12 4SQ
Contact Phone Nº: 07834 498205
Web Site: www.nairncountyfc.co.uk
E-mail: info@nairncountyfc.co.uk

GENERAL INFORMATION

Car Parking: Limited number of spaces adjoining the ground
Coach Parking: At the ground
Nearest Railway Station: Nairn (adjacent)
Nearest Bus Station: King Street, Nairn (½ mile)
Club Shop: At the ground
Opening Times: Matchdays only

GROUND INFORMATION

Away Supporters' Entrances & Sections:
No usual segregation

ADMISSION INFO (2017/2018 PRICES)

Adult Standing: £8.00
Adult Seating: £9.00
Senior Citizen/Child Standing: £5.00
Senior Citizen/Child Seating: £6.00
Note: Under-14s are admitted free with a paying adult
Programme Price: £2.00

DISABLED INFORMATION

Wheelchairs: Accommodated in the Stand
Helpers: Admitted
Prices: £5.00 for disabled fans
Disabled Toilets: Available
Contact: (01667) 454298   (Bookings are appreciated)

Travelling Supporters' Information:
Routes: The ground is situated on the south side of Nairn at Balblair Road, adjacent to the Railway Station.

ROTHES FC

Founded: 1938
Former Names: Rothes Victoria FC
Nickname: 'The Speysiders'
Ground: Mackessack Park, Station Street, Rothes, AB38 7BY
Ground Capacity: 1,731
Seating Capacity: 160
Record Attendance: 2,054 (September 1946)
Pitch Size: 108 × 74 yards

Colours: Tangerine shirts with Black shorts
Telephone Nº: 07821 192502 or 07827 774797 (Matchdays only)
Social Club Nº: (01340) 831348
Contact Address: Garry Davies, 87 Provost Christie Drive, Rothes AB38 7BU
Contact Phone Nº: (01340) 832314
Web site: www.rothesfc.co.uk
E-mail: rothesfc@highlandleague.com

GENERAL INFORMATION

Car Parking: At the ground
Coach Parking: At the ground
Nearest Railway Station: Elgin
Nearest Bus Station: Elgin
Club Shop: At the ground during home matches and also via the club's web site.

GROUND INFORMATION

Away Supporters' Entrances & Sections:
No usual segregation

ADMISSION INFO (2017/2018 PRICES)

Adult Standing: £8.00
Adult Seating: £9.00
Child Standing: £4.00
Child Seating: £5.00
Note: Under-14s are admitted free with a paying adult
Programme Price: £1.50

DISABLED INFORMATION

Wheelchairs: Accommodated
Helpers: Admitted
Prices: Normal prices apply
Disabled Toilets: Available

Travelling Supporters' Information:
Routes: From the A96 take the A941 signposted for Perth and follow into Rothes. After entering the town take the 2nd exit (A941 Perth) before immediately turning 1st left down a small track. Follow this past the distillery to reach the ground.

STRATHSPEY THISTLE FC

Founded: 1993
Former Names: None
Nickname: 'Thistle'
Ground: Seafield Park, Heathfield Road, Grantown-on-Spey   PH26 3HY
Ground Capacity: 1,500   **Seating Capacity**: 320
Pitch Size: 108 x 70 yards

Colours: Blue shirts with White shorts
Telephone Nº: None
Contact Address: Malky Taylor, Clunemore, Kinchurdy Road, Boat of Garten   PH24 3BP
Contact Phone Nº: (01479) 831233
Web site: www.strathspeythistlefc.co.uk

GENERAL INFORMATION
Car Parking: At the ground and nearby
Coach Parking: At the ground
Nearest Railway Station: Aviemore (14 miles)
Club Shop: None

GROUND INFORMATION
Away Supporters' Entrances & Sections: No usual segregation

ADMISSION INFO (2017/2018 PRICES)
Adult Standing: £8.00   **Adult Seating**: £8.00
Child Standing: £4.00
Child Seating: £4.00
Note: Under-14s are admitted free with a paying adult
Programme Price: £1.50

DISABLED INFORMATION
Wheelchairs: No special accommodation
Helpers: Admitted
Prices: Concessionary prices are charged for the disabled
Disabled Toilets: Available
Contact: (01479) 872277   (Bookings are not necessary)

Travelling Supporters' Information:
Routes: From Forres: Take the A939 to Grantown-on-Spey and upon entering town, take the 1st left then the 1st right into Heathfield Road. Continue along then turn 1st left into Golf Course Road and the ground is ¼ mile along the road.
From Aviemore: Take the A939 to Grantown-on-Spey and turn right at the first set of traffic lights into Woodside Avenue. Continue along the road for about ½ mile then turn right into Golf Course Road for the ground.

TURRIFF UNITED FC

Founded: 1954
Former Names: None
Nickname: 'Turra' or 'United'
Ground: The Haughs, Turriff   AB53 4ER
Ground Capacity: 2,135
Seating Capacity: 320
Record Attendance: 500
Pitch Size: 106 x 70 yards

Colours: Navy Blue shirts and shorts
Telephone Nº: (01888) 563486
Fax Number: (01888) 562909
Contact Address: Morgan Greig, 3 Craigwell Cottages, King Edward, Banff   AB45 3PT
Web site: www.turriffunited.co.uk

GENERAL INFORMATION
Car Parking: At the ground
Coach Parking: At the ground
Nearest Railway Station: Inverurie (20 miles)
Nearest Bus Station: Turriff
Club Shop: Available via the Club's web site only

GROUND INFORMATION
Away Supporters' Entrances & Sections:
No usual segregation

ADMISSION INFO (2017/2018 PRICES)
Adult Standing: £7.00
Adult Seating: £8.00
Child Standing: £4.00
Child Seating: £4.00
Note: Under-14s are admitted free with a paying adult
Programme Price: £1.50

DISABLED INFORMATION
Wheelchairs: Accommodated
Helpers: Admitted
Prices: Normal prices for the disabled and helpers
Disabled Toilets: Available
Contact: 07919 095322 (Bookings are necessary)

Travelling Supporters' Information:
Routes: From the North: Take the A947 to Turriff and, after the only roundabout in town, turn 1st right down to The Haughs. The ground is adjacent to the Swimming Pool.

WICK ACADEMY FC

Founded: 1893
Nickname: 'The Scorries'
Ground: Harmsworth Park, South Road, Wick, Caithness   KW1 5NH
Ground Capacity: 2,000
Seating Capacity: 433
Record Attendance: 2,000 (vs Hearts, 30th July 1984)

Pitch Size: 106 × 74 yards
Colours: Black and White striped shirts, Black shorts
Telephone N°: (01955) 602446
Fax Number: (01955) 602446
Correspondence: Jan Robertson, 5 Seaview Cottages, Dunnet Caithness   KW14 8XF
Web Site: www.wick-academy.co.uk

GENERAL INFORMATION

Car Parking: At the ground
Coach Parking: At the ground
Nearest Railway Station: Wick (10 minutes walk)
Nearest Bus Station: Wick
Club Shop: At Driftwood, River Street, Wick and also at Driftwood, Ormlie Industrial Estate
Opening Times: 9.00am to 5.00pm
Telephone N°: (01955) 602446

GROUND INFORMATION

Away Supporters' Entrances & Sections:
No usual segregation

ADMISSION INFO (2017/2018 PRICES)

Adult Standing: £800
Adult Seating: £8.00
Ages 12-16/Senior Citizen Standing: £4.00
Ages 12-16/Senior Citizen Seating: £4.00
Note: Under-12s are admitted free with a paying adult
Programme Price: £1.00

DISABLED INFORMATION

Wheelchairs: 2 spaces available in the North Stand
Helpers: Please phone the club for details
Prices: Please phone the club for details
Disabled Toilets: Available
Contact: (01955) 602446   (Bookings are necessary)

Travelling Supporters' Information:
Routes: The ground is situated on the A99 road from Inverness beside the Cemetery.

THE SCOTTISH LOWLAND FOOTBALL LEAGUE

Founded   2013

Web site   www.slfl.co.uk

<u>Clubs for the 2017/2018 Season</u>

BSC Glasgow FC .... Page 67

Civil Service Stollers FC .... Page 68

Cumbernauld Colts FC .... Page 69

Dalbeattie Star FC.. Page 70

East Kilbride FC .... Page 71

East Stirlingshire FC .... Page 72

Edinburgh University FC .... Page 73

Edusport Academy FC .... Page 74

Gala Fairydean Rovers FC .... Page 75

Gretna 2008 FC .... Page 76

Hawick Royal Albert FC .... Page 77

Selkirk FC... Page 78

The Spartans FC .... Page 79

University of Stirling FC .... Page 80

Vale of Leithen FC .... Page 81

Whitehill Welfare FC .... Page 82

BSC GLASGOW FC

The club are groundsharing with Alloa Athletic FC for the 2017/2018 season.

Founded: 2014
Nickname: 'The Baguettes'
Ground: The Indodrill Stadium, Clackmannan Road, Alloa FK10 1RY
Ground Capacity: 3,100 **Seating Capacity**: 900
Record Attendance: 13,000 (26th February 1939)
Pitch Size: 110 × 75 yards

Colours: Yellow shirts and shorts
Telephone Nº: (0141) 328-1503
Fax Number: (0141) 280-1234
Contact Address: G.Fraser, 44 Dykebar Avenue, Glasgow G13 3HF
Web Site: www.bscglasgow.co.uk
E-mail: mail@bscglasgow.co.uk

GENERAL INFORMATION

Car Parking: A Car Park is adjacent to the ground
Coach Parking: By Police Direction
Nearest Railway Station: Alloa
Nearest Bus Station: Alloa
Club Shop: None

GROUND INFORMATION

Away Supporters' Entrances & Sections:
Hilton Road entrance for the Hilton Road Side

ADMISSION INFO (2017/2018 PRICES)

Adult Standing/Seating: £7.00
Concessionary Standing/Seating: £3.00
Child Standing/Seating: £2.00

DISABLED INFORMATION

Wheelchairs: Accommodated
Helpers: One admitted per disabled supporter
Prices: Normal prices apply
Disabled Toilets: Available
Contact: (0141) 328-1503 (Bookings are not necessary)

Travelling Supporters' Information:
Routes: From the South and East: Take the M74 to the M80 and exit at Junction 9 following the A907 into Alloa. Continue over two roundabouts passing the brewery and Town Centre. The Ground is on the left-hand side of the road.

CIVIL SERVICE STROLLERS FC

Founded: 1908
Nickname: 'Strollers'
Ground: Civil Service Sports Ground, Marine Drive, Edinburgh
Ground Capacity: 500 approximately (no seating)
Record Attendance: Unknown
Pitch Size: 100 × 60 yards

Colours: White shirts with Black shorts
Telephone Nº: (0131) 332-1175
Fax Number: None
Contact Address: Keith Stewart,
117 Wester Broom Drive, Edinburgh   EH12 7RQ
Contact Phone Nº: 07402 521912
Web Site: www.csstrollers.com

GENERAL INFORMATION

Car Parking: At the ground
Coach Parking: At the ground
Nearest Railway Station: Edinburgh Waverley
Nearest Bus Station: St. Andrew's Square
Club Shop: None
Police Telephone Nº: (0131) 200-7211

ADMISSION INFO (2017/2018 PRICES)

Adult Standing: £5.00
Adult Seating: £5.00
Child Standing: £3.00
Child Seating: £3.00
Programme Price: None

DISABLED INFORMATION

Wheelchairs: Accommodated
Disabled Toilets: Available
Contact: –   (Bookings are not necessary)

Travelling Supporters' Information:
Routes: From the West: Take the A90 Queensferry Road into Edinburgh and continue until reaching the B9085 (Quality Street). Turn left into Quality Street and continue into Cramond Road. After ¼ mile turn right into Lauriston Farm Road. Continue to the roundabout and go left along Silver Knowes Road then into Marine Drive for the Ground; From the East: Take the A1 into Edinburgh and at the 1st roundabout take the 2nd exit into Milton Link. At the next roundabout (¼ mile) take 2nd exit onto A199 Sir Harry Lauder Road. Continue along A199 for approximately 2½ miles past Leith then join the A901 (Lindsay Road). Continue along A901 to the end of Lower Granton Road then take the 3rd exit at the roundabout into West Granton Road and after 1¼ mile take the 3rd exit at the roundabout into Marine Drive.

CUMBERNAULD COLTS FC

Founded: 1969 (**Entered League**: 2015)
Nickname: 'Colts'
Ground: Broadwood Stadium, Cumbernauld, Glasgow   G68 9NE
Ground Capacity: 8,200 (all seats)
Record Attendance: 8,000 (14th August 1996)
Pitch Size: 115 × 75 yards

Colours: Yellow Shirts with Blue shorts
Contact Address: Stewart McKenzie, 8 Lime Crescent, Cumbernauld   G67 3PQ
Telephone Nº: 07798 646110
Web Site: www.cumbernauldcoltsfc.com
E-mail: admin@cumbernauldcoltsfc.com

GENERAL INFORMATION
Car Parking: Behind the Main and West Stands
Coach Parking: Behind the Main Stand
Nearest Railway Station: Croy (1½ miles)
Nearest Bus Station: Cumbernauld Town Centre
Club Shop: None

GROUND INFORMATION
Away Supporters' Entrances & Sections:
No usual segregation

ADMISSION INFO (2017/2018 PRICES)
Adult Seating: £5.00
Concessionary Seating: £2.00
Note: Under-16s are admitted free with a paying adult

DISABLED INFORMATION
Wheelchairs: 10 spaces each for home and away fans accommodated in front sections of each stand
Helpers: One helper admitted per wheelchair
Prices: Please contact the club for information
Disabled Toilets: 4 available in the Main and West Stands
Contact: 07798 646110   (Bookings are not necessary)

Travelling Supporters' Information:
Routes: From all Parts: Exit the A80 at Broadwood Junction and follow the signs for Broadwood. The ground is signposted from the next roundabout.

DALBEATTIE STAR FC

Founded: 1905
Nickname: 'The Star'
Ground: Islecroft Stadium, Dalbeattie, Dumfries & Galloway DG5 4HE
Ground Capacity: 3,500
Seating Capacity: 300
Record Attendance: Not known

Pitch Size: 110 × 72 yards
Colours: Red and Black shirts, Black shorts
Contact Address: R.Geddes, 31 Alpine Street, Dalbeattie DG5 4HQ
Contact Phone Nº: (01556) 610563
Contact Mobile Nº: 07860 549444
Web Site: www.dalbeattiestar.co.uk

GENERAL INFORMATION
Car Parking: At the ground
Coach Parking: At the ground
Nearest Railway Station: Dumfries
Nearest Bus Station: Dalbeattie
Club Shop: None

GROUND INFORMATION
Away Supporters' Entrances & Sections:
No usual segregation

ADMISSION INFO (2017/2018 PRICES)
Adult Standing: £5.00
Adult Seating: £5.00
Child Standing: £3.00
Child Seating: £3.00
Concessionary Standing/Seating: £3.00
Programme Price: £1.00

DISABLED INFORMATION
Wheelchairs: Accommodated
Helpers: Admitted
Prices: Please contact the club for further information
Disabled Toilets: Available
Contact: (01556) 610 563   (Bookings are not necessary)

Travelling Supporters' Information:
Routes: Take the A711 from Dumfries to Dalbeattie. Upon entering Dalbeattie, turn left just before the Pheasant Hotel then first left and left again at the mini-roundabout for the ground.

EAST KILBRIDE FC

Founded: 2010
Nickname: 'The Kilby' or 'EK'
Ground: K Park Training Academy, Calderglen Country Park, East Kilbride   G75 0QZ
Ground Capacity: 400
Seating Capacity: 400
Record Attendance: 330 (2013/2014 season)

Pitch Size: 110 × 72 yards
Colours: Blue and Gold halved shirts, Blue shorts
Contact Address: Peter Hickey, 97 Glen Doll, St. Leonards, East Kilbride   G74 3SU
Contact Phone Nº: (01355) 225538
Contact Mobile Nº: 07757 859368
Web site: www.eastkilbridefootballclub.co.uk

GENERAL INFORMATION

Car Parking: At the ground
Coach Parking: At the ground
Nearest Railway Station: East Kilbride (2 miles)
Nearest Bus Station: East Kilbride (2 miles)
Club Shop: None

GROUND INFORMATION

Away Supporters' Entrances & Sections:
No usual segregation

ADMISSION INFO (2017/2018 PRICES)

Adult Standing: £6.00
Adult Seating: £6.00
Child Standing: £3.00
Child Seating: £3.00
Concessions Standing/Seating: £3.00
Programme Price: £1.00

DISABLED INFORMATION

Wheelchairs: Accommodated
Helpers: Admitted
Prices: Please contact the club for further information
Disabled Toilets: Available
Contact: (01355) 225538   (Bookings are not necessary)

Travelling Supporters' Information:
Routes: From the East: Take the A726 into East Kilbride after passing the East Kilbride Shopping Centre, continue straight on at the first roundabout then take the 2nd exit at the next roundabout onto Strathaven Road (still the A726). After a short distance, turn left into Calderglen Country Park at the brown tourist sign. From the South: Take the A726 northwards from Strathaven. Upon entering the outskirts of East Kilbride, turn right into Calderglen Country Park at the brown tourist sign. From the North and East: Take the A749/A725 to East Kilbride and follow the A725 towards the south of the town. Turn left onto the A726 signposted for Strathaven and follow a short distance before turning left into Calderglen Country Park.

EAST STIRLINGSHIRE FC

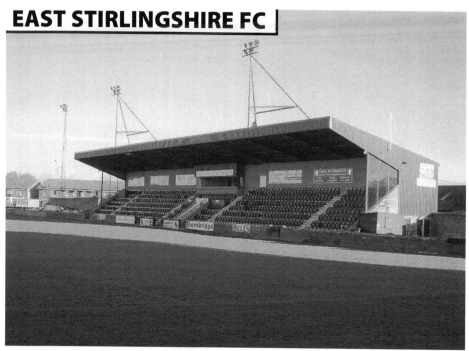

East Stirlingshire are groundsharing with Stenhousemuir for the 2017/2018 season.

Founded: 1880 (**Entered League**: 1900)
Former Names: Bainsford Britannia FC
Nickname: 'The Shire'
Ground: Ochilview Park, Gladstone Road,
Stenhousemuir FK5 5QL
Ground Capacity: 2,654
Seating Capacity: 628
Pitch Size: 110 × 72 yards

Record Attendance: 12,000 (21/2/1921 – Firs Park)
Colours: Black and White hooped shirts, Black shorts
Office Address: 1 South Broomage Avenue, Larbert,
FK5 3LD
Telephone Nº: (01324) 871171
Web Site: www.eaststirlingshirefc.co.uk
E-mail: fceaststirlingshire@gmail.com

GENERAL INFORMATION

Car Parking: A large Car Park is adjacent
Coach Parking: Behind the North Terracing
Nearest Railway Station: Larbert (1 mile)
Nearest Bus Station: Falkirk (2½ miles)
Club Shop: At the office (see above for details)
Opening Times: Weekdays from 9.00am to 3.00pm
Telephone Nº: (01324) 871171

GROUND INFORMATION

Away Supporters' Entrances & Sections:
No usual segregation

ADMISSION INFO (2017/2018 PRICES)

Adult Standing: £8.00
Adult Seating: £8.00
Concessionary Standing: £4.00
Concessionary Seating: £4.00
Programme Price: £2.00

DISABLED INFORMATION

Wheelchairs: Accommodated
Helpers: One helper admitted for each disabled fan
Prices: £5.00 for the disabled. Helpers admitted free.
Disabled Toilets: Available in the Main Stand
Contact: (01324) 871171 (Bookings are necessary)

Travelling Supporters' Information:
Routes: Exit the M876 at Junction 2 and follow signs for Stenhousemuir. Pass the Old Hospital and turn right after the Golf Course. The ground is on the left behind the houses – the floodlights are visible for ¼ mile.

EDINBURGH UNIVERSITY FC

Founded: 1878
Nickname: 'The Burgh'
Ground: East Peffermill Playing Field, 136 Peffermill Road, Edinburgh EH16 5LT
Ground Capacity: 1,000
Seating Capacity: 101
Record Attendance: 800
Pitch Size: 113 × 74 yards

Colours: Green shirts with Navy Blue shorts
Telephone Nº: (0131) 650-2346 (Sports Union) and 07542 352101 (Secretary)
Contact Address: Edinburgh University AFC, c/o Edinburgh University Sports Union, 48 Pleasance, Edinburgh EH8 9TJ
Web Site: www.euafc.com
E-mail: info@euafc.com

GENERAL INFORMATION
Car Parking: 30 spaces at the East Peffermill Car Park
Coach Parking: Available in the University grounds
Nearest Railway Station: Edinburgh Waverley (2¼ miles)
Nearest Bus Station: St. Andrew Square (2½ miles)
(Lothian Buses services 14, 30 & 42 all pass the ground)
Club Shop: None

GROUND INFORMATION
Away Supporters' Entrances & Sections:
No usual segregation

ADMISSION INFO (2017/2018 PRICES)
Adult Standing/Seating: £5.00
Child Standing/Seating: £3.00
Concessionary Standing/Seating: £3.00

DISABLED INFORMATION
Wheelchairs: 3 covered spaces available within the stand
Helpers: Admitted
Prices: Normal prices apply for the disabled. Free for helpers
Disabled Toilets: Available
Contact: (0131) 650-2346   (Bookings are not necessary)

Travelling Supporters' Information:
Routes: The most straightforward approach to the Peffermill facilities is from the Edinburgh City bypass on the south side of the city. Leave the Edinburgh City bypass at the Straiton juntion and head north towards the city on the A701 (Burdiehouse Road). After approximately 2½ miles turn right the traffic lights onto Lady Road, with the Cameron Toll Shopping Centre on your right hand side. Continue straight on at the small roundabout then take the second exit at the large roundabout on to the A6095 Peffermill Road. The entrance to playing fields on the right after ½ mile.   Coaches should drop off at the gates.

EDUSPORT ACADEMY FC

Edusport Academy FC are playing at Annan Athletic's Galabank ground during the 2017/2018 season.

Founded: 2011
Former Names: None
Nickname: None
Ground: Galabank, North Street, Annan, Dumfries & Galloway   DG12 5DQ
Pitch Size: 110 × 66 yards

Ground Capacity: 2,514
Seating Capacity: 474
Colours: Blue shirts with White shorts
Contact Address: 272 Bath Street, Glasgow G2 4JR
Web Site: www.edusportacademy.com

GENERAL INFORMATION
Car Parking: Available at the ground
Coach Parking: Available at the ground
Nearest Railway Station: Annan
Nearest Bus Station: Annan

GROUND INFORMATION
Away Supporters' Entrances & Sections:
North Stand

ADMISSION INFO (2017/2018 PRICES)
Adult Standing: £5.00
Adult Seating: £5.00
Child Standing: £3.00
Child Seating: £3.00

DISABLED INFORMATION
Wheelchairs: Accommodated
Helpers: Please phone the club for details
Prices: Please phone the club for details
Disabled Toilets: Available
Contact: (01461) 204108   (Bookings are necessary)

Travelling Supporters' Information:
Routes: From the East: Take the A75 to Annan. Approaching Annan, exit onto the B6357 (Stapleton Road) and after ¾ mile take the second exit at the roundabout into Scotts Street. Continue into Church Street and High Street. Turn right into Lady Street (B722) and following along into North Street for the ground; From the West: Take the A75 to Annan and turn right onto the B721 through Howes and into High Street in Annan (1 mile). After about 300 yards turn left into Lady Street. Then as above.

GALA FAIRYDEAN ROVERS FC

Founded: 1907
Nickname: 'The Braw Lads'
Ground: The 3G Arena, Nether Road, Netherdale, Galashiels TD1 3HE
Ground Capacity: 5,215
Seating Capacity: 460
Record Attendance: 6,000 (vs Rangers in 1989)
Pitch Size: 110 × 72 yards

Colours: Black and Red Striped shirts, White shorts
Ground Telephone Nº: None
Contact Address: Graeme McIver, St. Elmo, 3 Elm Row, Galashiels TD1 3JH
Contact Phone Nº: 07738 615562
Web Site: www.gfrfc.co.uk

GENERAL INFORMATION

Car Parking: Available at the ground
Coach Parking: Available at the ground
Nearest Railway Station: Galashiels (1½ miles)
Nearest Bus Station: Galashiels
Club Shop: None at present, but purchases can be made via the club's web site.

GROUND INFORMATION

Away Supporters' Entrances & Sections:
No usual segregation

ADMISSION INFO (2017/2018 PRICES)

Adult Standing: £5.00
Adult Seating: £5.00
Child Standing: Free of charge with a paying adult
Child Seating: Free of charge with a paying adult
Concessionary Standing/Seating: £2.00
Programme Price: £2.00

DISABLED INFORMATION

Wheelchairs: Accommodated
Helpers: Please phone the club for details
Prices: Please phone the club for details
Disabled Toilets: Available
Contact: 07738 615562 – Graeme McIver
(Bookings are not necessary)

Travelling Supporters' Information:
Routes: From Edinburgh: Take the A7 to Galashiels and follow signs for Heriot-Watt University and Netherdale. After passing the Fire Station on the left, turn-off left at the mini-roundabout along Tweed Road and the ground is ½ mile on the left; From Jedburgh/Hawick: Take the A7 to Galashiels and turn right at the mini-roundabout for the ground.

GRETNA 2008 FC

Founded: 2008
Nickname: 'Black and Whites'
Ground: Raydale Park, Dominion Road, Gretna, DG16 5AP
Ground Capacity: 1,030   **Seating Capacity**: 797
Record Attendance: 653 (2009)
Pitch Size: 112 × 74 yards

Colours: Black shirts with a White flash, Black shorts
Contact Address: Kevin Smith, 72 Melbourne Avenue, Eastriggs, Annan   DG12 6PG
Contact Telephone N°: (01461) 701062
Contact Mobile N°: 07902 826124
Web Site: www.gretnafc2008.co.uk

GENERAL INFORMATION
Car Parking: At the ground
Coach Parking: At the ground
Nearest Railway Station: Gretna Green (1 mile)
Nearest Bus Station: Carlisle (10 miles)
Club Shop: At the ground
Opening Times: Matchdays only
Telephone N°: –

GROUND INFORMATION
Away Supporters' Entrances & Sections:
West Enclosure

ADMISSION INFO (2017/2018 PRICES)
Adult Standing: £5.00
Adult Seating: £5.00
Child Standing: £1.00
Child Seating: £1.00
Programme Price: £1.50

DISABLED INFORMATION
Wheelchairs: Accommodated
Helpers: Admitted
Prices: Please contact the club for further information
Disabled Toilets: Available
Contact: 07902 824126   (Bookings are not necessary)

Travelling Supporters' Information:
Routes: From All Parts: Leave the A74 at the Gretna turn-off and exit onto the B7076. Cross Border Bridge with the Gretna Chase Hotel on the right then turn left at the Gretna Inn into Annan Road. After ¼ mile turn left into Dominion Road and the ground is on the right.

HAWICK ROYAL ALBERT FC

Founded: 1947
Nickname: 'The Royalists'
Ground: Albert Park, Mansfield Road, Hawick, TD9 8AW
Ground Capacity: 2,000
Seating Capacity: 500
Record Attendance: 3,000

Pitch Size: 100 × 68 yards
Colours: Royal Blue shirts and shorts
Contact Address: D. Purves, 16 Lanton Place, Hawick TD9 7QL
Contact Nº: 07862 295028
Web Site: www.hawickroyalalbert.co.uk

GENERAL INFORMATION

Car Parking: Available at the ground
Coach Parking: Available at the ground
Nearest Railway Station: Edinburgh or Carlisle
Nearest Bus Station: Hawick Centre
Club Shop: None
Police Telephone Nº: (01450) 375051

GROUND INFORMATION

Away Supporters' Entrances & Sections:
No usual segregation

ADMISSION INFO (2017/2018 PRICES)

Adult Standing: £5.00
Adult Seating: £5.00
Child Standing: £3.00
Child Seating: £3.00

DISABLED INFORMATION

Wheelchairs: Accommodated
Helpers: Admitted
Prices: Free of charge for the disabled
Disabled Toilets: Available
Contact: – (Bookings are not necessary)

Travelling Supporters' Information:
Routes: From the North: Take the A7 into Hawick. At the first set of traffic lights, turn left into Mansfield Road. Follow the river to the roundabout and take the 2nd exit. Albert Park is the third pitch, after the two Rugby pitches on the left; From the South: Take the A7 into Hawick and turn right into Mansfield Road, then as above.

SELKIRK FC

Founded: 1880
Nickname: 'Souters'
Ground: Yarrow Park, Ettrickhaugh Road, Selkirk, TD7 5AZ
Ground Capacity: 1,162
Seating Capacity: 100
Record Attendance: Not known

Pitch Size: 108 × 70 yards
Colours: Shirts & shorts are Royal Blue with White trim
Office Phone Nº: (01750) 778147
Contact Mobile Nº: 07984 984572 (Secretary)
Web Site: www.selkirkfc.com

GENERAL INFORMATION
Car Parking: Available at the junction of the A707 & A708 behind the Rugby club
Coach Parking: As above
Nearest Railway Station: Galashiels (from 2015 – 7 miles)
Nearest Bus Station: Selkirk
Club Shop: None

GROUND INFORMATION
Away Supporters' Entrances & Sections: No usual segregation

ADMISSION INFO (2017/2018 PRICES)
Adult Standing: £5.00
Adult Seating: £5.00
Child Standing: Free of charge
Child Seating: Free of charge
Programme Price: £2.00

DISABLED INFORMATION
Wheelchairs: Accommodated
Helpers: Please phone the club for details
Prices: Please phone the club for details
Disabled Toilets: 2 available in the club house
Contact: (01750) 21995 (Bookings are not necessary)

Travelling Supporters' Information:
Routes: From Edinburgh: Take the A7 to Selkirk. Turn right by the Monument in the market place and follow the road towards the river, cross the bridge into Ettrick Haugh Road and pass the Rugby ground. Take the next right towards the Cricket Club and continue along for 400 yards to the ground.

THE SPARTANS FC

Founded: 1951
Nickname: None
Ground: Ainslie Park, 94 Pilton Drive, Edinburgh, EH5 2HF
Telephone Nº: (0131) 552 7854
Ground Capacity: 3,500
Seating Capacity: 504

Record Attendance: 3,127 (vs Man United XI in 2011)
Pitch Size: 109 × 72 yards
Colours: White shirts with Red shorts and White socks
Contact Address: John McCabe, 72 Denholm Road, Musselburgh EH21 6TU
Contact Phone Nº: (0131) 665-8225
Web Site: www.spartansfc.com

GENERAL INFORMATION

Car Parking: At the ground
Coach Parking: At the ground by prior arrangement
Nearest Railway Station: Edinburgh Waverley (2¾ miles)
Nearest Bus Station: St. Andrew's Square
Club Shop: At the ground

GROUND INFORMATION

Away Supporters' Entrances & Sections:
No usual segregation. Enter through Ainslie Park Leisure Centre car park

ADMISSION INFO (2017/2018 PRICES)

Adult Standing: £7.00
Adult Seating: £7.00
Under-15s Standing: Free of charge
Under-15s Seating: Free of charge
Concessionary Standing/Seating: £3.00
Programme Price: £2.00

DISABLED INFORMATION

Wheelchairs: Accommodated
Helpers: Please check club's web site for details
Prices: Please check club's web site for details
Disabled Toilets: Available
Contact: (0131) 552-7854 (Bookings are not necessary)

Travelling Supporters' Information:
Routes: From the West: Take the A90 Queensferry Road into Edinburgh and continue until reaching the A902 (Telford Road). Turn left into Telford Road and take the 3rd exit at the roundabout into Ferry Road. Turn left into Pilton Drive immediately after passing the Morrisons Supermarket and enter the ground through Ainslie Park leisure centre; From the East: Take the A1 into Edinburgh and at the 1st roundabout take the 2nd exit into Milton Link and continue onto Sir Harry Lauder Road (A199). Continue along the A199 for approximately 2½ miles past Leith then turn left onto the A902 which continues into Ferry Road. Turn into Pilton Drive just before the Morrisons Supermarket, then as above.

UNIVERSITY OF STIRLING FC

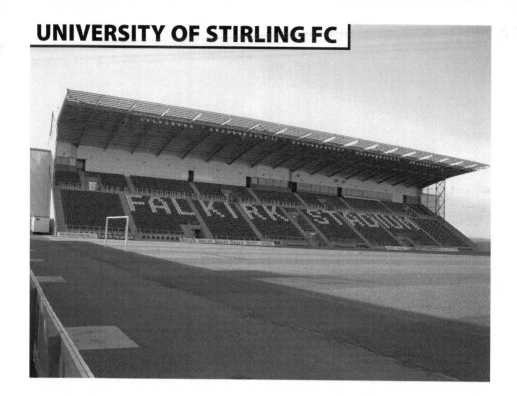

Founded: 2008
Nickname: None
Ground: The Falkirk Stadium, 4 Stadium Way, Falkirk FK2 9EE
Ground Capacity: 8,750 (All seats)
Pitch Size: 112 x 75 yards

Colours: Green shirts and shorts
Contact Address: Jason Atkins, Gannochy Sports Centre, University of Stirling, Stirling FK9 4LA
Contact Phone N°: (01786) 466553
Web site: www.stir.ac.uk/footballclub

GENERAL INFORMATION
Car Parking: A large Car Park is adjacent
Coach Parking: Available nearby
Nearest Railway Station: Falkirk Grahamston (1 mile)
Nearest Bus Station: Falkirk (1 mile)
Club Shop: None

GROUND INFORMATION
Away Supporters' Entrances & Sections:
No usual segregation

ADMISSION INFO (2017/2018 PRICES)
Adult Seating: £5.00
Child Seating: £3.00
Concessionary Seating: £3.00
Programme Price: £2.00

DISABLED INFORMATION
Wheelchairs: Accommodated
Helpers: Admitted
Prices: Please contact the club for details
Disabled Toilets: Available
Contact: 07740 500140   (Bookings are not necessary)

Travelling Supporters' Information:
Routes: Exit the M9 at Junction 6 and take the A904 towards Falkirk. Continue into Falkirk at the Westfield/Laurieston roundabout along Grangemouth Road and take the first right into Alexander Avenue. Then take the 2nd right into Westfield Street and the ground is on the right.

VALE OF LEITHEN FC

Founded: 1891
Nickname: 'Vale'
Ground: Victoria Park, Innerleithen
Ground Capacity: 1,500 (no seating)
Record Attendance: 3,500
Pitch Size: 108 × 70 yards

Colours: Navy Blue shirts and shorts
Contact E-mail: valeofleithen@slfl.co.uk
Web Site: www.valeofleithen.co.uk

GENERAL INFORMATION
Car Parking: Available at the ground
Coach Parking: Available at the ground
Nearest Railway Station: Edinburgh (29 miles)
Nearest Bus Station: Peebles
Club Shop: None

GROUND INFORMATION
Away Supporters' Entrances & Sections:
No usual segregation

ADMISSION INFO (2017/2018 PRICES)
Adult Standing: £5.00
Child Standing: £3.00
Concessionary Standing: £3.00
Programme Price: £2.00

DISABLED INFORMATION
Wheelchairs: Accommodated
Helpers: Please phone the club for details
Prices: Please phone the club for details
Disabled Toilets: Available opposite the ground
Contact: None   (Bookings are not necessary)

Travelling Supporters' Information:
Routes: Take the A72 to Innerleithen from Peebles. Upon entering Innerleithen, turn left into Hall Street at the crossroads for access to the ground.

WHITEHILL WELFARE FC

Founded: 1953
Nickname: 'The Welfare'
Ground: Ferguson Park, Carnethie Street, Rosewell, Midlothian   EH24 9DS
Ground Capacity: 2,614
Seating Capacity: 136
Record Attendance: 2,000 (vs Celtic)

Pitch Size: 110 × 66 yards
Colours: Shirts are Maroon with Sky Blue, White shorts
Contact Phone Nº: 07437 870555
Web Site: www.whitehillwelfare.co.uk
E-mail: whitehillwelfare@gmail.com

GENERAL INFORMATION

Car Parking: At the ground
Coach Parking: At the ground
Nearest Railway Station: Edinburgh Waverley (10 miles)
Nearest Bus Station: St. Andrew's Square, Edinburgh
Club Shop: None

GROUND INFORMATION

Away Supporters' Entrances & Sections:
No usual segregation

ADMISSION INFO (2017/2018 PRICES)

Adult Standing: £5.00
Adult Seating: £5.00
Child Standing: £3.00
Child Seating: £3.00
Concessionary Standing/Seating: £3.00
Programme Price: £1.00

DISABLED INFORMATION

Wheelchairs: Accommodated
Helpers: Please phone the club for details
Prices: Please phone the club for details
Disabled Toilets: Available
Contact: 07762 319639   (Bookings are not necessary)

Travelling Supporters' Information:
Routes: From Edinburgh: Take the A6094 into Rosewell. In Rosewell, turn left then left again opposite St. Matthews Roman Catholic Primary School. The ground is situated next to Ferguson Park Garage.

Scottish Premiership 2016/2017 Season	Aberdeen	Celtic	Dundee	Hamilton Academical	Heart of Midlothian	Inverness Cal. Thistle	Kilmarnock	Motherwell	Partick Thistle	Rangers	Ross County	St. Johnstone
Aberdeen		0-1	3-0	2-1	0-0	1-1	5-1	7-2	2-1	2-1	4-0	0-0
		1-3			2-0	1-0		1-0	2-0	0-3	1-0	0-2
Celtic	4-1		2-1	1-0	4-0	3-0	6-1	2-0	1-0	5-1	2-0	1-0
	1-0			2-0	2-0		3-1	2-0	1-1	1-1		4-1
Dundee	1-3	0-1		1-1	3-2	2-1	1-1	2-0	0-2	1-2	0-0	3-0
	0-7	1-2		0-2		0-2	1-1		0-1	2-1	1-1	
Hamilton Academical	1-0	0-3	0-1		3-3	1-1	1-2	1-1	1-1	1-2	1-0	1-1
	1-0		4-0				3-0	1-1	0-1		1-1	1-0
							0-2					
Heart of Midlothian	0-1	1-2	2-0	3-1		5-1	4-0	3-0	1-1	2-0	0-0	2-2
	1-2	0-5	1-0	4-0			1-1		2-2	4-1	0-1	
Inverness Caledonian Thistle	1-3	2-2	3-1	1-1	3-3		1-1	1-2	0-0	0-1	2-3	2-1
		0-4	2-2	2-1			1-1	3-2		2-1	1-1	0-3
Kilmarnock	0-4	0-1	2-0	0-0	2-0	1-1		1-2	2-2	1-1	3-2	0-1
	1-2		0-1		0-0	2-1		1-2	1-1	0-0	1-2	
Motherwell	1-3	3-4	0-0	4-2	1-3	0-3	0-0		2-0	0-2	4-1	1-2
			1-5	0-0	0-3	4-2	3-1				0-1	1-2
			2-3									
Partick Thistle	1-2	1-4	2-0	2-2	1-2	2-0	0-0	1-1		1-2	1-1	0-2
	0-6	0-5		2-0	2-0	1-1	1-0			1-2	2-1	0-1
Rangers	2-1	1-2	1-0	1-1	2-0	1-0	3-0	2-1	2-0		0-0	1-1
	1-2	1-5		4-0	2-1		1-1	2-0			1-1	3-2
Ross County	2-1	0-4	1-3	1-1	2-2	3-2	2-0	1-1	1-3	1-1		0-2
		2-2	2-1	3-2		4-0	1-2	1-2				1-2
St. Johnstone	0-0	2-4	2-1	3-0	1-0	3-0	0-1	1-1	1-2	1-1	2-4	
	1-2	2-5	2-0		1-0		0-2		1-0	1-2		
						1-0						

Scottish Premiership

Season 2016/2017

Celtic	38	34	4	0	106	25	106	Motherwell	38	10	8	20	46	69	38
Aberdeen	38	24	4	10	74	35	76	Dundee	38	10	7	21	38	62	37
Rangers	38	19	10	9	56	44	67	Hamilton Academical	38	7	14	17	37	56	35
St Johnstone	38	17	7	14	50	46	58	Inverness Caledonian Thistle	38	7	13	18	44	71	34
Heart of Midlothian	38	12	10	16	55	52	46								
Partick Thistle	38	10	12	16	38	54	42								
Ross County	38	11	13	14	48	58	46								
Kilmarnock	38	9	14	15	36	56	41								

With 5 games of the season left, the Premiership was split into two groups of 6. The top half contended for the title while the bottom half decided relegation.

Scottish Championship
2016/2017 Season

	Ayr United	Dumbarton	Dundee United	Dunfermline Athletic	Falkirk	Greenock Morton	Hibernian	Queen of the South	Raith Rovers	St. Mirren
Ayr United	■	4-4	0-1	0-0	0-1	2-1	0-3	1-0	0-2	1-1
	■	2-1	0-0	0-2	1-4	1-4	0-4	0-2	1-0	0-2
Dumbarton	0-3	■	1-0	2-2	2-1	0-2	0-1	0-0	0-0	1-1
	2-2	■	1-0	0-2	0-1	1-0	0-1	1-2	4-0	2-2
Dundee United	3-0	2-1	■	1-0	1-0	2-1	1-0	1-1	2-2	2-1
	2-1	2-2	■	1-0	1-1	1-1	0-1	3-3	3-0	3-2
Dunfermline Athletic	1-1	4-3	1-3	■	1-1	2-1	1-3	0-1	0-0	4-3
	0-1	5-1	1-1	■	1-2	3-1	1-1	1-1	1-0	1-1
Falkirk	2-0	1-0	3-1	2-1	■	1-1	1-2	2-2	2-4	3-1
	1-1	2-2	3-0	2-0	■	0-1	1-2	2-2	1-0	2-2
Greenock Morton	2-1	1-1	0-0	2-1	1-1	■	1-1	1-0	1-0	3-1
	1-1	2-1	1-1	0-1	2-2	■	1-1	1-0	2-0	1-4
Hibernian	1-2	2-0	1-1	2-1	1-1	4-0	■	4-0	1-1	2-0
	1-1	2-2	3-0	2-2	2-1	0-0	■	3-0	3-2	1-1
Queen of the South	4-1	1-2	1-4	2-2	2-0	0-5	0-0	■	3-1	2-3
	0-0	1-2	4-2	0-1	0-2	3-0	0-1	■	2-1	0-2
Raith Rovers	1-1	3-2	0-0	2-0	0-2	0-1	0-0	1-0	■	3-1
	2-1	1-3	2-1	0-2	1-4	2-0	1-1	1-1	■	2-0
St. Mirren	1-1	0-1	0-2	0-1	1-1	1-1	0-2	1-3	1-0	■
	6-2	1-1	3-2	0-0	1-2	1-1	2-0	0-3	5-0	■

Scottish Professional Football League Championship
Season 2016/2017

Hibernian	36	19	14	3	59	25	71
Falkirk	36	16	12	8	58	40	60
Dundee United	36	15	12	9	50	42	57
Greenock Morton	36	13	13	10	44	41	52
Dunfermline Athletic	36	12	12	12	46	43	48
Queen of the South	36	11	10	15	46	52	43
St Mirren	36	9	12	15	52	56	39
Dumbarton	36	9	12	15	46	56	39
Raith Rovers	36	10	9	17	35	52	39
Ayr United	36	7	12	17	33	62	33

84

Scottish League One 2016/2017 Season	Airdrieonians	Albion Rovers	Alloa Athletic	Brechin City	East Fife	Livingston	Peterhead	Queen's Park	Stenhousemuir	Stranraer
Airdrieonians		0-2	2-1	1-0	1-1	2-4	1-3	4-1	0-5	1-0
		1-2	0-1	3-1	2-2	0-4	4-1	3-2	1-0	1-2
Albion Rovers	1-2		0-4	0-2	1-0	0-1	0-1	2-0	4-0	3-2
	3-4		1-1	1-0	0-1	0-2	0-0	1-1	1-1	3-0
Alloa Athletic	1-2	0-0		1-2	2-1	1-3	4-0	1-1	4-1	2-2
	2-1	1-1		6-1	3-0	2-2	0-1	2-2	2-1	1-0
Brechin City	3-2	1-2	0-1		0-1	0-3	2-1	0-0	2-1	2-0
	3-0	1-0	1-2		2-1	0-2	0-1	3-1	2-2	0-0
East Fife	0-1	2-2	2-2	1-2		3-1	2-0	1-2	0-1	2-0
	0-4	2-0	0-0	3-2		2-1	1-2	0-0	1-0	0-0
Livingston	2-0	1-2	3-1	2-1	3-1		1-2	1-2	4-1	5-1
	4-2	3-0	2-1	3-0	0-1		4-1	4-0	1-0	0-0
Peterhead	2-4	2-2	1-1	1-3	0-3	1-2		2-0	0-2	2-0
	1-1	1-1	3-2	0-1	1-1	2-3		4-0	0-1	2-2
Queen's Park	1-3	2-1	1-2	2-0	1-0	1-0	0-0		0-3	0-2
	2-1	2-0	0-2	1-1	2-2	1-1	2-0		0-2	0-1
Stenhousemuir	2-2	1-0	2-2	1-3	0-1	0-4	2-2	1-2		0-5
	4-2	0-3	2-4	1-1	3-1	0-1	3-1	0-2		1-0
Stranraer	1-2	3-2	2-5	0-1	1-1	1-2	1-0	0-2	3-1	
	2-1	3-0	1-2	2-0	2-1	0-1	3-3	1-1	3-0	

Scottish Professional Football League
League One

Season 2016/2017

Team	P	W	D	L	F	A	Pts
Livingston	36	26	3	7	80	32	81
Alloa Athletic	36	17	11	8	69	44	62
Airdrieonians	36	16	4	16	61	66	52
Brechin City	36	15	5	16	43	49	50
East Fife	36	12	10	14	41	44	46
Queen's Park	36	12	10	14	37	51	46
Stranraer	36	12	8	16	46	50	44
Albion Rovers	36	11	9	16	41	48	42
Peterhead	36	10	10	16	44	59	40
Stenhousemuir	36	11	6	19	45	64	39

Scottish League Two 2016/2017 Season	Annan Athletic	Arbroath	Berwick Rangers	Clyde	Cowdenbeath	Edinburgh City	Elgin City	Forfar Athletic	Montrose	Stirling Albion
Annan Athletic		1-2	3-1	3-2	2-0	1-1	1-0	1-2	2-3	3-2
		2-5	2-1	1-0	1-0	1-0	1-0	1-2	5-1	4-1
Arbroath	1-1		1-1	4-0	0-0	0-1	3-2	2-0	0-0	5-3
	1-2		4-1	1-0	4-1	0-1	3-2	0-1	0-1	1-1
Berwick Rangers	2-0	1-1		1-1	1-1	1-3	2-4	1-2	1-2	3-2
	4-1	0-2		4-3	1-3	3-2	0-1	3-2	0-1	0-1
Clyde	2-3	3-2	3-2		5-3	0-0	2-1	0-1	2-1	1-1
	2-1	1-2	1-1		0-2	3-1	3-2	2-2	1-2	2-3
Cowdenbeath	2-2	0-2	0-2	1-0		2-0	0-1	3-4	2-0	0-2
	0-1	1-2	0-1	1-0		1-2	1-1	1-1	0-2	0-2
Edinburgh City	1-0	3-3	1-2	0-1	1-1		1-2	2-3	0-1	2-0
	2-0	0-2	2-2	0-0	1-1		3-0	0-1	1-1	1-0
Elgin City	0-2	0-1	6-0	0-2	3-1	3-0		2-2	4-1	2-3
	3-2	0-0	2-2	4-1	0-0	3-1		1-1	1-1	2-2
Forfar Athletic	5-1	0-1	2-0	4-3	4-3	1-1	3-2		1-3	4-1
	2-4	1-1	2-3	3-0	3-1	1-2	1-1		0-0	1-1
Montrose	2-2	1-1	0-0	2-1	1-2	0-1	0-5	1-1		2-2
	2-3	1-3	2-1	1-1	2-1	3-0	0-3	1-0		1-3
Stirling Albion	3-1	2-2	0-0	1-1	1-2	1-1	0-4	0-3	2-0	
	1-0	1-1	2-2	3-0	0-3	1-0	1-0	0-3	1-2	

Scottish Professional Football League League Two

Season 2016/2017

Arbroath	36	18	12	6	63	36	66
Forfar Athletic	36	18	10	8	69	49	64
Annan Athletic	36	18	4	14	61	58	58
Montrose	36	14	10	12	44	53	52
Elgin City	36	14	9	13	67	47	51
Stirling Albion	36	12	11	13	50	59	47
Edinburgh City	36	11	10	15	38	45	43
Berwick Rangers	36	10	10	16	50	65	40
Clyde	36	10	8	18	49	64	38
Cowdenbeath	36	9	8	19	40	55	35

86

	Brora Rangers	Buckie Thistle	Clachnacuddin	Cove Rangers	Deveronvale	Formartine United	Forres Mechanics	Fort William	Fraserburgh	Huntly	Inverurie Loco Works	Keith	Lossiemouth	Nairn County	Rothes	Strathspey Thistle	Turriff United	Wick Academy
Brora Rangers		2-1	6-0	1-2	6-2	5-0	3-0	8-0	2-0	2-0	2-2	6-0	7-0	3-3	5-0	4-3	2-1	2-0
Buckie Thistle	5-0		4-0	1-0	3-0	3-1	3-0	4-2	1-1	7-0	3-1	6-0	6-0	2-1	3-0	9-0	4-0	1-0
Clachnacuddin	0-5	1-5		2-2	2-1	0-2	2-4	2-2	3-2	1-1	2-0	1-2	2-0	1-0	2-1	0-2	0-0	0-0
Cove Rangers	2-1	2-3	3-2		2-0	5-1	3-2	7-0	2-2	6-0	3-0	3-0	5-0	2-1	5-0	4-0	0-0	6-0
Deveronvale	1-2	2-9	5-1	0-2		2-3	0-2	4-2	1-2	0-2	0-3	3-2	0-0	2-2	5-0	7-2	0-1	0-2
Formartine United	1-4	0-0	2-1	1-1	1-0		2-2	4-2	4-0	8-0	2-1	5-2	1-0	2-0	6-1	2-1	3-2	0-3
Forres Mechanics	1-2	3-2	2-2	0-3	2-1	0-0		4-0	0-2	2-1	1-1	4-1	4-2	7-1	1-1	2-0	1-4	3-5
Fort William	1-5	2-5	0-5	2-6	1-2	1-1	2-6		0-3	2-5	1-4	2-3	1-4	1-2	3-5	4-1	3-2	3-8
Fraserburgh	2-0	2-5	3-3	2-2	3-0	0-1	2-3	3-2		2-0	1-0	1-3	0-4	3-3	2-1	3-0	3-0	1-1
Huntly	1-6	1-0	0-2	0-8	5-2	3-3	0-3	5-1	2-4		2-1	2-1	0-0	4-6	2-1	2-2	2-4	1-5
Inverurie Loco Works	2-2	1-1	4-1	2-3	2-0	1-2	4-3	3-0	1-5	2-1		3-3	2-2	1-0	6-0	3-0	0-2	1-3
Keith	1-4	3-2	6-1	0-3	4-0	1-4	3-2	7-2	2-6	4-1	1-6		4-1	0-1	2-1	5-2	1-0	2-1
Lossiemouth	4-1	2-5	2-3	1-6	0-2	1-3	1-2	5-0	1-2	2-2	1-0	4-1		0-0	1-2	4-1	2-0	1-2
Nairn County	0-4	3-8	1-2	2-5	1-2	0-2	4-4	5-0	0-2	2-1	2-3	1-1	2-1		3-0	0-2	1-2	1-2
Rothes	0-6	1-6	2-2	0-1	2-1	1-5	0-5	2-1	0-5	2-2	2-2	4-2	0-2	0-2		4-2	1-4	0-9
Strathspey Thistle	0-5	2-9	1-4	1-1	0-3	1-6	1-3	0-1	0-7	0-2	1-7	0-4	1-2	2-2	0-1		0-2	0-3
Turriff United	0-1	2-2	4-2	1-1	2-1	1-2	3-4	4-0	1-0	2-0	0-1	3-2	2-0	2-0	2-1	2-0		1-0
Wick Academy	1-2	1-2	3-1	2-3	2-2	2-2	2-2	2-0	0-1	4-4	1-1	3-1	1-2	1-5	1-1	3-0	2-0	

Highland Football League

Season 2016/2017

Buckie Thistle	34	26	4	4	130	36	82
Cove Rangers	34	25	7	2	109	30	82
Brora Rangers	34	26	3	5	116	36	81
Formartine United	34	22	7	5	82	47	73
Fraserburgh	34	19	6	9	77	48	63
Forres Mechanics	34	17	7	10	84	63	58
Turriff United	34	18	4	12	56	42	58
Wick Academy	34	15	8	11	75	52	53
Inverurie Loco Works	34	14	8	12	71	53	50
Keith	34	15	2	17	74	88	47
Clachnacuddin	34	11	8	15	53	77	41
Lossiemouth	34	11	5	18	52	70	38
Nairn County	34	9	7	18	57	74	34
Huntly	34	9	7	18	54	97	34
Deveronvale	34	9	3	22	51	75	30
Rothes	34	7	5	22	37	106	26
Fort William	34	3	2	29	44	136	11
Strathspey Thistle	34	2	3	29	28	120	9

Lowland Football League 2016/2017 Season	BSC Glasgow	Civil Service Strollers	Cumbernauld Colts	Dalbeattie Star	East Kilbride	East Stirlingshire	Edinburgh University	Gala Fairydean Rovers	Gretna 2008	Hawick Royal Albert	Preston Athletic	Selkirk	Spartans	University of Stirling	Vale of Leithen	Whitehill Welfare
BSC Glasgow	■	2-1	1-1	2-3	1-1	0-6	0-0	2-3	2-0	3-1	8-3	1-1	1-2	4-1	2-0	3-0
Civil Service Strollers	3-1	■	1-1	4-2	1-1	3-8	2-1	3-3	1-2	0-5	3-1	5-2	2-2	1-2	2-4	0-2
Cumbernauld Colts	4-3	1-0	■	3-0	0-2	3-3	2-0	1-1	1-3	1-1	5-0	1-2	2-0	0-3	1-3	2-1
Dalbeattie Star	3-2	2-2	2-0	■	0-3	2-2	1-2	2-0	1-3	7-1	2-3	5-1	4-3	0-1	2-0	2-0
East Kilbride	3-1	4-0	0-1	3-0	■	1-0	2-0	3-1	3-0	2-1	4-0	6-0	2-0	5-0	4-2	4-1
East Stirlingshire	3-0	3-3	4-1	2-1	3-2	■	1-1	3-0	5-0	3-1	6-2	5-0	1-4	4-1	2-2	3-0
Edinburgh University	1-3	0-0	2-0	0-1	0-4	0-1	■	0-1	3-4	2-1	4-0	3-2	0-0	1-3	1-1	2-0
Gala Fairydean Rovers	2-1	3-2	2-2	2-4	1-6	1-10	1-3	■	1-0	5-1	3-1	1-1	3-2	2-2	4-2	2-3
Gretna 2008	1-3	0-4	1-1	1-0	1-5	0-3	0-0	1-1	■	2-0	5-3	1-1	0-3	0-3	3-0	3-1
Hawick Royal Albert	2-3	2-5	4-3	2-4	2-4	2-4	4-3	4-1	1-3	■	3-0	4-3	0-4	0-1	3-1	2-3
Preston Athletic	1-1	3-4	0-2	1-4	0-5	1-7	0-3	3-4	1-2	2-1	■	3-2	0-2	4-3	0-3	0-2
Selkirk	4-0	1-3	1-3	3-1	2-2	7-4	2-3	7-1	1-2	0-3	0-3	■	0-6	2-4	6-0	2-4
Spartans	2-1	3-1	0-1	1-2	1-0	1-0	1-1	1-1	4-1	9-1	2-1	3-0	■	0-1	2-2	2-0
University of Stirling	1-1	2-1	2-2	0-0	1-3	0-2	1-0	1-0	4-2	7-2	5-3	3-3	0-3	■	0-4	3-0
Vale of Leithen	2-6	1-2	1-2	1-1	1-2	2-4	1-0	2-3	3-1	4-3	3-1	2-1	1-6	0-1	■	2-1
Whitehill Welfare	1-5	4-0	0-3	2-2	0-3	2-5	1-3	5-3	0-1	3-1	4-1	3-1	1-0	4-0	0-2	■

Scottish Lowland Football League

Season 2016/2017

East Kilbride	30	24	3	3	89	21	75
East Stirlingshire	30	21	5	4	107	43	68
Spartans	30	17	5	8	69	30	56
Stirling University	30	16	5	9	60	53	53
Dalbeattie Star	30	14	5	11	60	50	47
Cumbernauld Colts	30	13	8	9	51	43	47
BSC Glasgow	30	12	6	12	63	56	42
Whitehill Welfare	30	13	1	16	53	64	40
Gretna 2008	30	12	4	14	44	65	40
Gala Fairydean Rovers	30	11	7	12	55	77	40
Edinburgh University	30	10	7	13	40	42	37
Civil Service Strollers	30	10	7	13	59	68	37
Vale of Leithen	30	11	4	15	52	66	37
Hawick Royal Albert	30	8	1	21	58	93	25
Selkirk	30	6	5	19	58	86	23
Preston Athletic	30	5	1	24	41	102	16

Scottish Cup 2016/2017

Round	Date	Home	Score	Away	Score
Round 1	24th Sep 2016	Turiff United	1	Bonnyrigg Rose	1
Round 1	24th Sep 2016	Fort William	1	Brora Rangers	4
Round 1	24th Sep 2016	Forres Mechanics	2	Lossiemouth	2
Round 1	24th Sep 2016	East Kilbride	9	Vale of Leithen	1
Round 1	24th Sep 2016	BSC Glasgow	3	Rothes	1
Round 1	24th Sep 2016	Deveronvale	0	Gretna 2008	3
Round 1	24th Sep 2016	Keith	0	Banks O' Dee	1
Round 1	24th Sep 2016	Edinburgh University	0	Whitehill Welfare	1
Round 1	24th Sep 2016	Gala Fairydean Rovers	3	Fraserburgh	1
Round 1	24th Sep 2016	Beith Juniors	6	Strathspey	0
Round 1	24th Sep 2016	Civil Service Strollers	1	Hawick Royal Albert	1
Round 1	24th Sep 2016	Nairn County	2	Preston Athletic	3
Round 1	24th Sep 2016	Inverurie Loco Works	0	Buckie Thistle	6
Round 1	24th Sep 2016	Clachnacuddin	1	Stirling University	2
Round 1	24th Sep 2016	Dalbeattie Star	1	Wick Academy	3
Round 1	24th Sep 2016	Selkirk	0	Linlithgow Rose	3
Round 1	24th Sep 2016	Girvan	1	Huntly	2
Round 1	25th Sep 2016	Leith Athletic	0	Cumbernauld Colts	0
Replay	1st Oct 2016	Bonnyrigg Rose	4	Turiff United	1
Replay	1st Oct 2016	Hawick Royal Albert	6	Civil Service Strollers	2
Replay	1st Oct 2016	Lossiemouth	0	Forres Mechanics	4
Replay	5th Oct 2016	Cumbernauld Colts	1	Leith Athletic	0
Round 2	22nd Oct 2016	Annan Athletic	0	East Stirlingshire	0
Round 2	22nd Oct 2016	Banks O' Dee	2	Formartine United	2
Round 2	22nd Oct 2016	Brora Rangers	0	Clyde	2
Round 2	22nd Oct 2016	BSC Glasgow	0	Beith Juniors	1
Round 2	22nd Oct 2016	Bonnyrigg Rose	2	Cove Rangers	1
Round 2	22nd Oct 2016	Berwick Rangers	2	Hawick Royal Albert	3
Round 2	22nd Oct 2016	Linlithgow Rose	0	Stirling Albion	3
Round 2	22nd Oct 2016	Wick Academy	4	Whitehill Welfare	1
Round 2	22nd Oct 2016	Preston Athletic	0	Montrose	3
Round 2	22nd Oct 2016	Huntly	0	Spartans	2
Round 2	22nd Oct 2016	Edinburgh City	0	Forfar Athletic	0
Round 2	22nd Oct 2016	Cowdenbeath	0	East Kilbride	1
Round 2	22nd Oct 2016	Cumbernauld Colts	2	Forres Mechanics	2
Round 2	22nd Oct 2016	Arbroath	3	Stirling University	1
Round 2	22nd Oct 2016	Gala Fairydean Rovers	0	Elgin City	4
Round 2	22nd Oct 2016	Buckie Thistle	1	Gretna 2008	1
Replay	29th Oct 2016	East Stirlingshire	1	Annan Athletic	2
Replay	29th Oct 2016	Formartine United	7	Banks O' Dee	2
Replay	29th Oct 2016	Forres Mechanics	4	Cumbernauld Colts	0
Replay	29th Oct 2016	Gretna 2008	2	Buckie Thistle	6
Replay	1st Nov 2016	Forfar Athletic	0	Edinburgh City	1
Round 3	26th Nov 2016	Bonnyrigg Rose	0	Dumbarton	0
Round 3	26th Nov 2016	Elgin City	8	Hawick Royal Albert	1
Round 3	26th Nov 2016	Airdrieonians	1	Livingston	2
Round 3	26th Nov 2016	Buckie Thistle	3	Dunfermline Athletic	5
Round 3	26th Nov 2016	Forres Mechanics	2	Stenhousemuir	2
Round 3	26th Nov 2016	Peterhead	0	Alloa Athletic	1
Round 3	29th Nov 2016	Queen's Park	2	Montrose	0
Round 3	29th Nov 2016	Albion Rovers	2	Queen of the South	1

Round 3	29th Nov 2016	East Fife	1	Edinburgh City	1	
Round 3	29th Nov 2016	Brechin City	0	Ayr United	1	
Round 3	29th Nov 2016	St Mirren	5	Spartans	1	
Round 3	3rd Dec 2016	Beith Juniors	0	Greenock Morton	6	
Round 3	3rd Dec 2016	Stirling Albion	2	Wick Academy	0	
Round 3	3rd Dec 2016	Stranraer	2	East Kilbride	1	
Round 3	3rd Dec 2016	Formartine United	4	Annan Athletic	0	
Round 3	6th Dec 2016	Clyde	5	Arbroath	0	
Replay	3rd Dec 2016	Stenhousemuir	3	Forres Mechanics	1	
Replay	6th Dec 2016	Dumbarton	0	Bonnyrigg Rose	1	
Replay	7th Dec 2016	Edinburgh City	0	East Fife	1	
Round 4	21st Jan 2017	Rangers	2	Motherwell	1	
Round 4	21st Jan 2017	Ross County	6	Dundee United	2	
Round 4	21st Jan 2017	St Johnstone	2	Stenhousemuir	0	
Round 4	21st Jan 2017	Livingston	0	East Fife	1	
Round 4	21st Jan 2017	Aberdeen	4	Stranraer	0	
Round 4	21st Jan 2017	Kilmarnock	0	Hamilton Academical	1	
Round 4	21st Jan 2017	Bonnyrigg Rose	1	Hibernian	8	
Round 4	21st Jan 2017	Ayr United	0	Queen's Park	0	
Round 4	21st Jan 2017	Partick Thistle	4	Formartine United	0	
Round 4	21st Jan 2017	Stirling Albion	2	Clyde	2	
Round 4	21st Jan 2017	Alloa Athletic	2	Dunfermline Athletic	3	
Round 4	21st Jan 2017	Dundee	0	St Mirren	2	
Round 4	21st Jan 2017	Greenock Morton	2	Falkirk	0	
Round 4	21st Jan 2017	Elgin City	1	Inverness Caledonian Thistle	2	
Round 4	22nd Jan 2017	Raith Rovers	1	Heart of Midlothian	1	
Round 4	22nd Jan 2017	Albion Rovers	0	Celtic	3	
Replay	24th Jan 2017	Queen's Park	2	Ayr United	2	(aet)
		Ayr United won 5-4 on penalties				
Replay	25th Jan 2017	Heart of Midlothian	4	Raith Rovers	2	(aet)
Replay	31st Jan 2017	Clyde	3	Stirling Albion	2	
Round 5	11th Feb 2017	Celtic	6	Inverness Caledonian Thistle	0	
Round 5	11th Feb 2017	Dunfermline Athletic	1	Hamilton Academical	1	
Round 5	11th Feb 2017	St Johnstone	0	Partick Thistle	1	
Round 5	11th Feb 2017	Ayr United	1	Clyde	1	
Round 5	11th Feb 2017	East Fife	2	St Mirren	3	
Round 5	11th Feb 2017	Ross County	0	Aberdeen	1	
Round 5	12th Feb 2017	Heart of Midlothian	0	Hibernian	0	
Round 5	12th Feb 2017	Rangers	2	Greenock Morton	1	
Replay	14th Feb 2017	Clyde	1	Ayr United	2	(aet)
Replay	14th Feb 2017	Hamilton Academical	1	Dunfermline Athletic	1	(aet)
		Hamilton Academical won 3-0 on penalties				
Replay	22nd Feb 2017	Hibernian	3	Heart of Midlothian	1	
Quarter-final	4th Mar 2017	Rangers	6	Hamilton Academical	0	
Quarter-final	4th Mar 2017	Hibernian	3	Ayr United	1	
Quarter-final	5th Mar 2017	Celtic	4	St Mirren	1	
Quarter-final	5th Mar 2017	Aberdeen	1	Partick Thistle	0	
Semi-final	22nd Apr 2017	Hibernian	2	Aberdeen	3	
Semi-final	23rd Apr 2017	Celtic	2	Rangers	0	
FINAL	27th May 2017	Celtic		Aberdeen		

Scottish League Cup 2016/2017

Group Stage North Section Group A	Peterhead	East Fife	Dundee	Forfar Athletic	Dumbarton
Peterhead			2-1	2-0	
East Fife	2-1		1-1 (4-2p)		
Dundee				7-0	6-2
Forfar Athletic		2-0			2-2 (5-3p)
Dumbarton	3-3 (5-6p)	0-2			

Group Stage North Section Group B	St. Johnstone	Falkirk	Stirling Albion	Brechin City	Elgin City
St. Johnstone		3-0	4-0		
Falkirk				2-0	3-0
Stirling Albion		1-0			4-1
Brechin City	1-1 (4-2p)		2-1		
Elgin City	1-3			4-2	

Group Stage – North Section

The top team in each group progressed to the Second Round and the four best runners-up between the 8 groups also progressed.

In the event of a draw, a penalty shootout for a bonus point took place (the results of these are shown in the grids).

In the tables below, PW indicates a penalty shoot-out win and a bonus point, PL indicates a shoot-out loss.

Group A	Pld	W	PW	PL	L	GF	GA	Pts
Peterhead	4	2	1	0	1	8	6	8
East Fife	4	2	1	0	1	5	4	8
Dundee	4	2	0	1	1	15	5	7
Forfar Athletic	4	1	1	0	2	4	11	5
Dumbarton	4	0	0	2	2	7	13	2

Group B	Pld	W	PW	PL	L	GF	GA	Pts
St. Johnstone	4	3	0	1	0	11	2	10
Falkirk	4	2	0	0	2	5	4	6
Stirling Albion	4	2	0	0	2	6	7	6
Brechin City	4	1	1	0	2	5	8	5
Elgin City	4	1	0	0	3	6	12	3

Group C	Pld	W	PW	PL	L	GF	GA	Pts
Inverness Caledonian Thistle	4	3	0	1	0	15	3	10
Dundee United	4	2	2	0	0	10	3	10
Dunfermline Athletic	4	2	0	0	2	7	7	6
Cowdenbeath	4	1	0	0	3	4	11	3
Arbroath	4	0	0	1	3	1	13	1

Group D	Pld	W	PW	PL	L	GF	GA	Pts
Alloa Athletic	4	4	0	0	0	10	2	12
Raith Rovers	4	2	1	0	1	5	4	8
Ross County	4	2	0	1	1	11	4	7
Cove Rangers	4	1	0	0	3	4	13	3
Montrose	4	0	0	0	4	1	8	0

Group Stage North Section Group C	Inverness Cal. Thistle	Dundee United	Dunfermline Athletic	Cowdenbeath	Arbroath
Inverness CT		1-1 (1-4p)			7-0
Dundee United			2-0	6-1	
Dunfermline Athletic	1-5				3-0
Cowdenbeath	1-2		0-3		
Arbroath		1-1 (3-5p)		0-2	

Group Stage North Section Group D	Alloa Athletic	Raith Rovers	Ross County	Cove Rangers	Montrose
Alloa Athletic			3-2	4-0	
Raith Rovers	0-1				2-1
Ross County		1-1 (3-4p)		7-0	
Cove Rangers		1-2			3-0
Montrose	0-2		0-1		

Group Stage South Section Group E	Partick Thistle	Queen of the South	Airdrieonians	Queen's Park	Stenhousemuir
Partick Thistle	■	2-1		2-0	
Queen of the South		■	2-0		1-0
Airdrieonians	0-1		■		2-1
Queen's Park		0-2	3-3 (7-8p)	■	
Stenhousemuir	1-4			0-2	■

Group Stage South Section Group F	Rangers	Motherwell	Stranraer	Annan Athletic	East Stirlingshire
Rangers	■		3-0	2-0	
Motherwell	0-2	■			3-0
Stranraer		0-3	■		3-1
Annan Athletic		1-3	1-2	■	
East Stirlingshire	0-3			0-2	■

South Section

The top team in each group progressed to the Second Round and the four best runners-up between the 8 groups also progressed.

In the tables below, PW indicates a penalty shoot-out win and a bonus point, PL indicates a shoot-out loss.

Group E	Pld	W	PW	PL	L	GF	GA	Pts
Partick Thistle	4	4	0	0	0	9	2	12
Queen of the South	4	3	0	0	1	6	2	9
Airdrieonians	4	1	1	0	2	5	7	5
Queen's Park	4	1	0	1	2	5	7	4
Stenhousemuir	4	0	0	0	4	2	9	0

Group F	Pld	W	PW	PL	L	GF	GA	Pts
Rangers	4	4	0	0	0	10	0	12
Motherwell	4	3	0	0	1	9	3	9
Stranraer	4	2	0	0	2	5	8	6
Annan Athletic	4	1	0	0	3	4	7	3
East Stirlingshire	4	0	0	0	4	1	11	0

Group G	Pld	W	PW	PL	L	GF	GA	Pts
Hamilton Academical	4	3	0	0	1	10	5	9
Ayr United	4	3	0	0	1	5	2	9
St Mirren	4	3	0	0	1	7	5	9
Livingston	4	1	0	0	3	6	7	3
Edinburgh City	4	0	0	0	4	2	11	0

Group H	Pld	W	PW	PL	L	GF	GA	Pts
Greenock Morton	4	3	1	0	0	5	0	11
Kilmarnock	4	2	0	1	1	5	5	7
Clyde	4	1	1	0	2	4	5	5
Albion Rovers	4	0	2	1	1	1	2	5
Berwick Rangers	4	0	0	2	2	3	6	2

Group Stage South Section Group G	Hamilton Academical	Ayr United	St. Mirren	Livingston	Edinburgh City
Hamilton Academ.	■		3-0	2-1	
Ayr United	2-1	■			1-0
St. Mirren		1-0	■		3-0
Livingston		0-2	2-3	■	
Edinburgh City	2-4			0-3	■

Group Stage South Section Group H	Greenock Morton	Kilmarnock	Clyde	Albion Rovers	Berwick Rangers
Greenock Morton	■		1-0		2-0
Kilmarnock	0-2	■		0-0 (3-5p)	
Clyde		1-2	■		1-1 (6-5p)
Albion Rovers	0-0 (3-4p)		1-2	■	
Berwick Rangers		2-3		0-0 (4-5p)	■

The four runners-up with the best record progressed to the Second Round:

Best runners-up	Pld	W	PW	PL	L	GF	GA	Pts
Dundee United	4	2	2	0	0	10	3	10
Motherwell	4	3	0	0	1	9	3	9
Queen of the South	4	3	0	0	1	6	2	9
Ayr United	4	3	0	0	1	5	2	9
Raith Rovers	4	2	1	0	1	5	4	8
East Fife	4	2	1	0	1	5	4	8
Kilmarnock	4	2	0	1	1	5	5	7
Falkirk	4	2	0	0	2	4	4	6

Round 2	9th Aug 2016	Alloa Athletic	1	Inverness Caledonian Thistle	0	
Round 2	9th Aug 2016	Rangers	5	Peterhead	0	
Round 2	9th Aug 2016	Dundee United	3	Partick Thistle	1	
Round 2	9th Aug 2016	Hamilton Academical	1	Greenock Morton	2	
Round 2	9th Aug 2016	Hibernian	1	Queen of the South	3	
Round 2	10th Aug 2016	Celtic	5	Motherwell	0	
Round 2	10th Aug 2016	St. Johnstone	3	Heart of Midlothian	2	
Round 2	10th Aug 2016	Ayr United	1	Aberdeen	2	
Quarter-final	20th Sep 2016	Greenock Morton	2	Dundee United	1	
Quarter-final	20th Sep 2016	Rangers	5	Queen of the South	0	
Quarter-final	21st Sep 2016	Celtic	2	Alloa Athletic	0	
Quarter-final	22nd Sep 2016	Aberdeen	1	St. Johnstone	0	
Semi-final	22nd Oct 2016	Greenock Morton	0	Aberdeen	2	
Semi-final	23rd Oct 2016	Rangers	0	Celtic	1	
FINAL	27th Nov 2016	Aberdeen	0	Celtic	3	

Scottish Challenge Cup 2016/2017

The competition was expanded to include two guest teams from Northern Ireland, two guest teams from Wales, four teams from the Highland Football League, four teams from the Lowland Football League and the Under-20 sides of the Scottish Premier League clubs.

First Round – North Section

Round 1	2nd Aug 2016	Ross County Under-20s	2	Brora Rangers	3	(aet)
Round 1	2nd Aug 2016	Inverness Caledonian Thistle U-20s	0	Arbroath	3	
Round 1	2nd Aug 2016	East Stirlingshire	0	Montrose	3	
Round 1	2nd Aug 2016	Stirling Albion	2	Heart of Midlothian Under-20s	3	
Round 1	2nd Aug 2016	St. Johnstone Under-20s	1	Turriff United	2	
Round 1	2nd Aug 2016	Formartine United	2	Aberdeen Under-20s	5	
Round 1	2nd Aug 2016	Cove Rangers	2	Dundee Under-20s	1	

First Round – South Section

Round 1	2nd Aug 2016	Clyde	0	Partick Thistle Under-20s	5	
Round 1	2nd Aug 2016	Celtic Under-20s	5	Annan Athletic	1	
Round 1	2nd Aug 2016	Berwick Rangers	0	Spartans	3	
Round 1	2nd Aug 2016	Motherwell Under-20s	2	Edinburgh City	1	
Round 1	2nd Aug 2016	Queen's Park	5	Kilmarnock Under-20s	2	
Round 1	3rd Aug 2016	Cumbernauld Colts	0	Hamilton Academical Under-20s	3	
Round 1	10th Aug 2016	Rangers Under-20s	4	Stirling University	0	

Second Round – North Section

Round 2	16th Aug 2016	Aberdeen Under-20s	1	Forfar Athletic	3	
Round 2	16th Aug 2016	Brechin City	4	Cove Rangers	1	
Round 2	16th Aug 2016	Elgin City	2	Heart of Midlothian Under-20s	0	
Round 2	16th Aug 2016	Peterhead	3	Brora Rangers	2	
Round 2	17th Aug 2016	Turriff United	1	Montrose	0	
Round 2	17th Aug 2016	Arbroath	2	East Fife	3	(aet)

Second Round – South Section

Round 2	16th Aug 2016	Partick Thistle Under-20s	1	Queen's Park	1	(aet)
		Queen's Park won 6-5 on penalties.				
Round 2	16th Aug 2016	Stranraer	7	Spartans	1	
Round 2	16th Aug 2016	Albion Rovers	2	Hamilton Academical Under-20s	0	
Round 2	16th Aug 2016	Motherwell Under-20s	1	Airdrieonians	2	
Round 2	16th Aug 2016	Cowdenbeath	1	Celtic Under-20s	2	
Round 2	17th Aug 2016	Rangers Under-20s	1	Stenhousemuir	3	

Third Round – North Section

Round 3	3rd Sep 2016	Alloa Athletic	3	East Fife	0	
Round 3	3rd Sep 2016	Brechin City	1	Dunfermline Athletic	5	
Round 3	3rd Sep 2016	Dundee United	3	Peterhead	2	(aet)
Round 3	3rd Sep 2016	Falkirk	6	Elgin City	1	
Round 3	3rd Sep 2016	Forfar Athletic	3	Raith Rovers	2	
Round 3	4th Sep 2016	Turriff United	0	Hibernian	3	

Third Round – South Section

Round 3	3rd Sep 2016	Albion Rovers	3	St. Mirren	4	(aet)
Round 3	3rd Sep 2016	Queen of the South	7	Stenhousemuir	1	
Round 3	3rd Sep 2016	Queen's Park	2	Greenock Morton	0	
Round 3	3rd Sep 2016	Stranraer	1	Dumbarton	0	
Round 3	3rd Sep 2016	Livingston	5	Celtic Under-20s	1	
Round 3	4th Sep 2016	Ayr United	3	Airdrieonians	2	(aet)
Round 4	7th Oct 2016	Crusaders	1	Livingston	2	Void
		The result was declared void and a replay was ordered after it emerged that Livingston had fielded an ineligible player.				
Round 4	7th Oct 2016	Ayr United	1	Falkirk	0	(aet)
Round 4	8th Oct 2016	Bala Town	2	Alloa Athletic	4	
Round 4	8th Oct 2016	Stranraer	0	Dundee United	1	
Round 4	8th Oct 2016	Forfar Athletic	1	The New Saints	3	
Round 4	8th Oct 2016	Hibernian	1	St. Mirren	2	
Round 4	8th Oct 2016	Dunfermline Athletic	2	Queen's Park	1	
Round 4	9th Oct 2016	Queen of the South	2	Linfield	0	(aet)
Replay	1st Nov 2016	Crusaders	0	Livingston	3	
Quarter-final	12th Nov 2016	Dunfermline Athletic	0	Dundee United	1	
Quarter-final	12th Nov 2016	Queen of the South	2	Alloa Athletic	0	
Quarter-final	13th Nov 2016	St. Mirren	2	Ayr United	1	
Quarter-final	13th Nov 2016	Livingston	0	The New Saints	3	
Semi-final	18th Feb 2017	Queen of the South	2	Dundee United	3	
Semi-final	19th Feb 2017	St. Mirren	4	The New Saints	1	
FINAL	25th Mar 2017	Dundee United	2	St. Mirren	1	